Photo Art & Craft

Carolyn Vosburg Hall

Published by

Krause Publications
700 East State St.
Iola, WI 54990-001
www.krause.com

Please call or write for our free catalog of publications. Our toll-free number to place an order or to obtain a free catalog is 800-258-0929 or please use our regular business telephone, 715-445-2214.

Photography by Carolyn Vosburg Hall, unless otherwise noted.
All project designs by Carolyn Vosburg Hall, unless otherwise noted.
Manufactured in the United States of America.

Library of Congress Cataloging-in-Publication Data

ISBN 0-87341-972-3
LC 2001086340

Cover photos and title page photo by Carolyn Vosburg Hall

Photo by Robert Vigiletti

For "Circus Clown and Elephant," Robert Vigiletti scanned a transparency into a computer, manipulated the colors and textures, and then ink-jet printed it on watercolor paper.

Thanks to:

I dedicate this book to artist-photographer Robert Vigiletti who has given me endless assistance over the years. "Get canned-air to blow dust off your negatives," he'd say, or "Have you tried Kodalith® film for dropping out gray values?" or recently "They are developing new computer printers with waterproof archival quality inks." When he did photography for my books, he always generously instructed me in lighting, depth of field in focusing, or film types along the way.

Thanks also to photographer Gunnar George who hired me at age 16 to work in his portrait studio to tint photographs and let me experiment in the darkroom, exploring the mysteries of creating photographs.

Thanks to relatives and friends who served as models for pictures shown. Thanks to creative artists who allowed their works to be shown in the book. Thanks to the folks at Krause who made this book a reality.

Foreword

By Robert Vigiletti

Since the invention of photography by Louis Daguerre in 1839, artists and laypeople have toiled to find an appropriate use for this modern visual medium. We have discovered that photography has extremely widespread, useful applications. It is used effectively in advertising, documenting people, places and events, reporting news, and more. Although somewhat controversial, I feel safe in saying that photography has finally been accepted as fine art, that is: self-expression unto itself. Furthermore, photography can be employed in conjunction with other established art forms, craft forms, and today's electronic media. It is with these last three mentioned applications of photography that this book is so richly involved.

Carolyn Vosburg Hall, artist and author of twelve successful books on arts and crafts, presents information in a manner that stimulates creativity through projects that are doable by anyone who is willing to try. She introduces several techniques that combine photography with other art and craft media as well as techniques to manipulate the photographic image itself. There are simple projects that make it easy for the novice to get started, as well as more complicated projects for those who like greater challenges. In any case, the information is clearly presented and directed toward the pleasure one gets from the accomplishment of a creative project.

Photo by Robert Vigiletti

For "Egg," Vigiletti freed the fragile emulsion from a Polaroid photo and gently transferred it to the surface of an egg.

Vigiletti is the founder of the Photography Department at Center for Creative Studies in Detroit, Michigan. He also served as department chairman and interim dean of academic affairs.

Table of Contents

Show off your travel or garden pictures by adhering them to wood blocks or tiles for coasters.

Celebrate a special occasion by making a photo label including the honoree's picture.

It takes photos in two poses to make a jumping-jack toy.

Using polymer clay that bakes in the oven, you can model anybody, then add a photo face.

Make a photo quilt from a prized collection.

Use your computer to manipulate photos for note cards.

Cameras used in this book: Minolta®, Nikon®, Olympus®, Kodak®, Polaroid®
Films: Kodak, Fuji, Polaroid
Photography shops: World Camera, PhotoFast, Pro Photo, Wolf Camera, Ritz
All photography by Carolyn Vosburg Hall, unless otherwise noted.

Introduction

What can you make with photos?

A "mirror with a memory" is what people called those first magical photographs in the mid 1800s. Before the invention of the camera—which led to the photocopier, computer, scanner, digital camera, camcorder, and more—you had to spend hours drawing or painting to save a scene. Now there's easy access to many ways to create, collect, and save photo imagery to use in making art and craft objects.

What can you make? More than fifty projects show how to use photographic imagery to create imaginative artworks and novel craft objects. To begin, you can make note cards, postcards, place cards, and gift cards or assemble imaginative scrapbooks. Move on to transferring images to various materials such as fabric for quilt blocks, glass, canvas, or wood. You can create artwork to frame or construct objects—blocks, toys, lamps, and sculpture. Further, you can put images into your computer to make booklets, birthday cards, banners, and more.

What's in the drawer? Look at the identity photo on the front to see. This idea works for labeling key racks, hat and coat pegs, cupboards, or even cans of food.

Shoot photos of your collection, such as masks, and transfer the photos to fabric to make an art quilt.

Photo Art & Craft

Who can do these projects? Anyone can use one or another idea, since there is no need to know how to draw or use a darkroom. With common tools and techniques you can use images of family members, pets, favorite objects, scenes, or other images to create useful, artistic, decorative or experimental objects.

Where did the book idea come from? As a 10-year-old, I won a small camera in the Fourth of July foot race. Lacking film, I drew several small pictures and popped them in the camera. "Want your picture?" I'd ask friends, then snap, open the camera, and hand them a drawing. They liked it! Since then, I have used photo imagery to create wall hangings, wooden and paper toys, metal sculpture, framed pictures, screen prints, photocopied holiday cards, and other creations. I try everything.

Where are supplies obtained? Continuous in-

Decorate your table with your own photo creations.

vention in products and technology gives you a world of materials and techniques to try, all available in stores or catalogs. Projects list materials, sources, and references for more information. This is an idea book. Now you can try everything, too.

Make a wooden pull toy from an enlarged photo of your pet. Jessie cat is shown here.

Chapter One

Using photos and photocopies

10

13

17

19

21

23

26

28

30

32

some projects use ac-
tual photographs glued or sewn
directly on art or craft objects.
However, if you wish to preserve the originals, you can duplicate them in various ways—
printing from the negative,
re-photographing, photocopying, or digitizing. You can tuck
the original photo back in your
album and use this copy to trim,
cut out, glue on, frame, or manipulate.

Photocopying is the most
common duplicating process
suggested in these projects.
Photocopiers can enlarge or reduce the size of your original
photo. They can improve the
clarity, contrast, and archival
quality of old photos, newspaper articles, old letters, pages
from the family bible, and
other valuable memorabilia.
Copy machines print on ordinary office paper, colored
paper, and various textured papers from glossy to handmade.
The copy can be used for transfer techniques that will not
work on photographic emulsion papers. Photocopies have
permanent color unlike the
water-soluble ink used in computer printers, so you can use
them in more ways.

Modern copy machines can
print full rich colors, change the
size, flip the image, and more.
Inside the machine, the image
is separated into four colors—a
coating of vinyl dust in each
color is laid on and then heated
to fuse the particles into a
water-resistant photocopy.
Sometimes the machines can't

"read" photos well and strange
copies come out. Try placing a
sheet of white paper behind
photos to ease this problem.
Ask the store attendant about
any such oddities of their machines. If their machine cannot
make good copies, go elsewhere
to a better-maintained machine.

The thickness of copy paper
is noted by weight on the package label (for example, standard is 20-24 pounds). Other
information is given such as rag
content, recycled, surface texture, and color. Many copiers
will not take heavier or textured papers.

Color copy machines are
now easy enough for customers
to operate them. This takes a
bit of practice to estimate the
amount of enlargement or re-
duction to achieve the size you
want. The 100% mark means
the photo will be copied to size.
Enlarged 200%, the copy will be
twice as long, twice as high, and
four times the area. At 400%,
enlargement dimensions increase four times and area in-
creases sixteen times. You may
only get part of the photograph.

Copies usually show a white
border around the edges. The
print will run off the edges
when the copy size chosen is
larger than the paper or the
paper is not oriented with the
print. Be sure to place the
photo horizontal or vertical,
consistent with the paper as
shown on the control board.
On some projects, you can save
money by ganging prints—
placing several photos on one

Start with ribbons and a jar lid to make
an "old time" badge to celebrate a special event such as Lois and Jack
Goodrich's 50th wedding anniversary.

sheet of paper to be copied
then trimmed apart. Details
about different ways to use
photocopies are included in the
projects.

Don't forget your original in
the copier.

Note: Professional photographs are copyrighted and
cannot be copied without permission. The artist-photographer's profession is based on
his/her selective eye and photographic skill. Enjoy taking
and using your own photos.

Memory photo box

The author and her sister Lois Vosburg Goodrich at ages six and four, photocopied from an old photo.

One of the easiest ways to store your photos is in a shoe-sized storage box with a slot for identification on the front and divider cards inside. Available in photo stores, the boxes are covered with various decorative papers, so you can use an already-covered box or decorate your own. Be sure to date and identify each photograph on the back in non-smear ink, and tuck the negatives packet in the box. Someone doing a genealogy search in years to come will thank you.

Affix a nostalgic photo to the top to remember what's in the box. Photocopy the image, enlarged to size, to simulate an old print. You can use a black and white home photocopier to print the image on tan paper for an antique effect.

You need:

- Cardboard photo box 8" x 11 1/2" x 4 1/2"
- Old photo
- Tan paper 8 1/2" x 11"
- Border: Black paper 8" x 12"
- Scissors or paper cutter
- Glue stick

Start with an old photo, a photo storage box, backing paper, and clear laminate covering to make a nostalgic memory box.

Photo Art & Craft

1 Select a photo that indicates what's stored in the box. Set the photocopy machine to enlarge. Shown is a 400% enlargement of a selected photo area. This means a 3" photo enlarged four times is 12". To simulate an old print, copy the photo in black on tan paper.

2 Use a box that is covered with decorative paper, or choose a plain box and cover it yourself.

3 Trim the border paper with a paper cutter or scissors to fit the box top, and glue it in place. Trim the photo so the border shows all around, and glue on the photo.

4 Partly peel the backing from the laminate sheet, and carefully unroll it onto the photo. No second chances. It sticks! It will tear up the surface if you try to reposition it. Rub the adhered laminate firmly to complete the seal. Unstuck spots will appear gray.

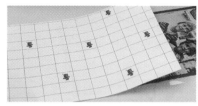

Clear plastic laminating sheets protect and waterproof photocopies and photographs.

5 Fold the laminate over the box sides. Clip the corners, fold the tabs on the box, and fold the ends down over them.

Side view of a complete box.

Sources: Any enlarging copier (home copier Xerox® B/W XD100 used here); Avery™ glue stick; JM Laminating Sheets 9" x 12"

A Hall photo album, circa 1875, holds family tintypes and early photographs, which someone had the good sense to identify.

Got some great photos?

Glue them on note cards and send them to friends.

Photo by Douglas Stroud

Put a favorite photo on your computer screen (see chapter 6).

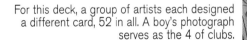

For this deck, a group of artists each designed a different card, 52 in all. A boy's photograph serves as the 4 of clubs.

Photo Tip 6 *You've got pictures!*

We've had cameras to record people, scenes, and events for the past 150 years. By now you probably have boxes, drawers, and albums full of pictures—a wonderful treasure trove of images to use. These photos of family and friends, of special places, and half-remembered events are probably all tucked away from sight. This will help preserve them for archival purposes (photos ultimately will fade), but how about giving some of them greater visibility? One old lady puts a photo in with every bill she pays, since she doesn't know what else to do with her life-long assortment. Now is the time to organize your photos to use and enjoy.

Photo Art & Craft

A photo page by Magali deVulpilliers. The horizontal photo album measures 9" x 12".

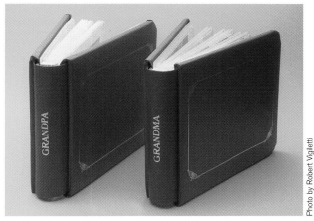
Karen Vigiletti Mallon made special grandma and grandpa albums to honor her parents.

Photo by Robert Vigiletti

Memory books

Examples by Magali deVulpilliers and Karen Vigiletti Mallon

A rich supply of materials is available for presenting album photos in context in lively fashion. Pages from Magali deVulpilliers' photo albums show inventive layouts. Even when she places photos squarely on the page, she embellishes them with titles and identification using the newsman's litany of who, what, why, where, and when. Handwritten titles show up well on black if pens with pigmented, colored inks are used. Titles clipped from magazines and ads can achieve humorous effect.

Some memory books emphasize a theme. Karen Vigiletti Mallon made grandfather and grandmother books for her parents. Using photos taken on family camping trips, vacations, zoo trips, and other precious moments, she composed the books as carefully as storybooks, documenting the child's growth and leading the viewer to a final burst of affection for the grandparents.

Karen's small albums, about 6" x 8", have room for one photo with descriptive works and colorful stickers on each page.

Photo by Robert Vigiletti

You need:

- Photo album
- Photos
- Archival glue
- Pens with opaque ink
- Scissors
- Source for lettering

Albums come in wondrous variety—a large format such as Magali's or smaller ones like Karen's. Oversized or horizontal albums don't fit easily in standard bookcases, but you can group them together.

Paper pages come in various weights and colors—black, off white, or colored—or in plastic covered, "magnetic" pages. Some albums have removable pages to work on flat or to add more pages.

The great surge of interest in memory books has brought a vast assortment of albums, stickers, glues, and instructions to crafters.

Karen's books show how memory books can record the many good times families share.

1 Take a full roll or two of film at each event, wedding, birthday party, or trip for a better range of activities and more chance for great candid shots. Choose the best, and tuck away or toss out the bad ones. Then group related pictures on the pages, or devote an entire album to one event or trip.

2 Arrange the photos with an eye to over-all page design. In Figure 1, Magali aligns photos squarely, and then tilts a few to enliven the page. Or she cuts out the figures and overlaps them to resemble a blooming bouquet (Figure 2).

3 Cut out along the figure outline, or tear out random shapes. Make additional copies from the negatives or the originals if you don't want to cut up your photos.

4 Add color to black and white photo pages with cutouts, stickers, and titles.

Figure 1. For clear writing, use a colored gel pen with opaque ink to write on dark photo backgrounds or colored photo pages.

Figure 2. For a dynamic look, Magali cut out the photographs of the young man featured, eliminating unnecessary backgrounds. By clustering the photos, she burst him to prominence.

Photo Art & Craft

5 Use a glue that is easy to apply, one that will not harm the photo, and a flexible one that will last. Or use small, colored paper corners (archival mounting corners), neutral pH adhesive, or photo tabs (Infinity Quick-stick photo tabs). Look for acid free, non-yellowing adhesives.

Sources: For paper and adhesives: Dick Blick Art Materials® catalog 1-800-447-8192, Michaels®, photo shops, crafts stores. For more ideas, try these titles also published by Krause Publications: *Ultimate Scrapbook Guide* by Julie Stephani; *More Than Memories III* by Julie Stephani; *Memory Crafting* by Judi Kauffman; *Pages* by Linda Fry Kenzle; *The Crafter's Guide to Glues* by Tammy Young.

Bright colored papers can enhance the photos, but keep colors subtle to feature the photos.

Magali deVulpilliers creates lively photo albums on black and white pages in horizontal format with a leatherette cover.

You can clip headlines from magazines and newspapers to add comments to album pages. Lots of stickers are now available for enhancing photo pages.

Black and white photos are enlivened with red rose stickers.

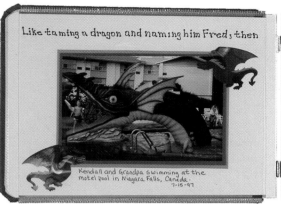

Like taming a dragon and naming him Fred, then

Kendall and Grandpa swimming at the motel pool in Niagara Falls, Canada. 7-15-97

Kendall and Grandpa at the Great Sand Dunes in Colorado 7-27-95

walking through sand dunes with hats on our heads.

Photo by Robert Viglietti

Photo Tip

Making albums

For people who always want ways to store their precious photographs safely, yet show them off to advantage, photo albums are the most common choice. Some early albums were clad in tooled-leather covers with slotted, pasteboard frames for tintype photos. Descendants of early album owners are lucky if someone labeled the photos. Album making is enormously popular today, and those you make will become valuable keepsakes of tomorrow.

How you stick the photos in the album becomes a major issue. Photographs are vulnerable to light fading and other damages. Over the years the wrong glue (mucilage or rubber cement), heat, dampness, and acid in paper can deteriorate photos. Use special glues that will not deteriorate the surface. Choose archival quality, acid-free paper pages for best results. Store your albums in a cool dry place. Albums with plastic envelope pages allow you to remove the photos, but be sure to replace them.

This typical leather-bound photo album from 1875, has thick slotted page holdings for photographs and brass clasps to close it securely.

Tintype photos called for long film exposure times, requiring the subject to sit sternly still at length.

Magali deVulpilliers photographs nostalgic scenes of her hometown Williamsburg to sell in gift shops, neatly packaged with envelopes.

Suzanne Vosburg Sherado embellished a favorite old photo in three different ways for note cards.

Simon Layton chooses the photograph he took of his first car as imagery for his note cards.

Photo note cards

Examples by Magali de Vulpilliers, Suzanne Sherado, and Simon Layton

Feature any kind of imagery you like on your card—people, places, pets, or parties. The photo can cover the entire card, show a narrow border, or be placed off center. Try your photo on a variety of background colors and textures to see which gives the most sizzle. Unusual handmade papers are available at art supply stores to make cards. On a dark-colored card, use a lighter insert paper for your message or use a colored pen with opaque ink. Consider choosing the envelope before or during selection of the note card size and paper. Art and office supply stores sell quality note cards with matching envelopes.

Add any decorative objects that will create the mood of the image—colored mats, ribbons, stickers, hand-painted designs, stamped images, pressed flowers, coins, or pieces of candy. If you get too crazy here, you will need to check with the post office and perhaps write "hand cancel" on the envelope.

You need:
- Photo 3" x 5" or 4" x 6"
- Note card (cover stock or hand-made paper)
- Note card envelope (standard is 5 1/4" x 7 1/4")
- Added decoration
- Glue stick

1 Select a photograph to feature. Make the note card the size and shape to suit your photo. A folded 5" x 7" card will take a 4" x 6" or 3" x 5" photo. Or begin with a standard size envelope to design your cards.

2 Trim the photo to eliminate extraneous imagery or to focus the scene.

3 Glue the photo to the card or to a colored paper frame. Then add details to this tiny artwork such as your signature or the location.

4 For a postcard, back the photo with adhesive paper available in kits or make your own paper.

5 To make your own envelope:

A. Use paper at least twice the size of the card. Remember that odd-sized, square, or lumpy envelopes must be hand-canceled and require additional postage.

B. Lay the card diagonally on the paper, trace the outline, and fold up the edges. Unfold and trim so the edges overlap. Glue the overlap (only) of three flaps. Insert your card, fold down the fourth overlap, and glue or sticker it shut.

C. Or lay the card straight on the envelope paper, leaving a 2" flap at the top. Fold in the sides, and fold up the bottom to 1 1/2" from the top. Unfold and trim the flaps to allow for 1/2" overlap. Glue the side flaps.

Sources: Avery glue stick; Photo A La Carte postcard kit (8 blanks in 3" x 5" or 4" x 6" sizes). Also published by Krause Publications: *Arnold Grummer's Guide to Easy Papermaking* by Arnold Grummer.

Photo Tip

Sharing pictures

To share your photos with friends, make your own cards or purchase postcard kits with adhesive backing to adhere your favorite photo and send it off. You can show your photos in small albums, in frames, on holiday cards, or pin them on a bulletin board in your kitchen for all to see. Some people prefer a framed formal arrangement; others stick up new shots of family and friends wherever there's space. "It's like having everyone there with you," Lois Goodrich says of her picture wall.

Lois Goodrich pins up a new photo on her giant bulletin board the minute it arrives.

Dave Goodrich treats his photo wall formally, choosing a special frame for each photo and designing the entire wall.

A related Florida scene best fit this palm frame.

Palm frame

The palm photo used for covering the frame focuses in close, making the fronds into an over-all pattern like wallpaper. To begin, photocopy your photo to size. Unlike computer printouts, photocopy colors are waterproof so they can be used in a variety of ways. You can cover a wooden frame like the palm frame, or make a copy the size of the frame's glass and inset a featured photo over it. In the double photo (below), Brent Hood smiles in front of the beach he loves. You can add a paper mat behind the photo to isolate and emphasize it.

For this frame, pop out the plastic glass to change photos from the front. Background Photo by Dr. Robert Vosburg.

You need:
- Photo 4" x 6" or 3" x 5"
- Unfinished wooden frame (shown is 8" x 10" with a 4" x 6" opening)
- Photocopy, 11" x 17" or large enough to cover the frame plus sides
- Paper or felt backing

Supplies and tools:
Ruler, mat cutter, No. 2 pencil, white glue, scotch tape, roller, paintbrush and water, sponge, right angle triangle, acrylic paint, water-based polyurethane

1 Choose a photo with an over-all design that won't overwhelm the photo in the frame, and photocopy it to 11" x 17", the largest many color copies can do. Use two copies pieced for a larger frame.

Choose a patterned photocopy to cover a ready-made frame.

2 Place the photocopy over the frame, in front of light, to select the best part of the design. On the photocopy back, trace the outside and opening edges of the frame with pencil.

Hold the frame behind the photocopy to silhouette it for selecting the best part of the design.

To cover a frame, trace the frame edges and center opening.

3 Fold the photocopy over the frame to score the paper. Add 1/2" to the photocopy for folding onto the frame back. Trim the corners.

4 On the opening, draw right angle lines inward from each corner and down the center. Cut these lines to the inside corners, and fold down on the opening edges.

Trim along the traced pattern lines and fold the photocopy up over the frame to crease the paper.

5 Paint the frame-opening's inside corner edges with a matching color, where the paper will not cover. Let dry.

6 Dilute white glue to paint the photocopy back. Align the photocopy on the frame, and press or roll it with the glue bottle to push out all air bubbles. Fold down the two side edges and roll them.

7 Glue the corners to the frame top and bottom, then glue the top and bottom edges over them. Glue all edges onto the frame back, and tape in place to hold.

8 Sponge off the surface glue and let dry.

9 Varnish the frame with polyurethane.

10 Measure and cut a paper or felt backing to cover the back of the frame. Cut out the inside opening. Glue on the backing and roll out all bubbles.

Sources: Michaels, Office Max®, Kinko's®

Photo Tip *Framing photos*

A frame does several things. It displays the photo and isolates it from background clutter. A glassed frame protects a photo from dust, moisture, wear, and light fading. UV glass protects against fading better than non-glare glass, which obscures detail. Use a frame with a removable backing to allow for changing the photo, or a narrow 'front-loading' frame that pops the clear plastic "glass" out to change photos.

In choosing a frame, relate the frame to the photo and avoid overwhelming the photo with busy frame imagery. This palm frame design is so strong that only the photo shown held its own. Choose a frame to emphasize and feature the photo. Frame groupings are popular now, almost like a cluster of friends standing by.

Photo Art & Craft

Wolf Camera in Sarasota made this 16" x 24" photo poster from a 4" x 6" photo.

Posters

Bigger can be better

Sometimes you can't tell what a wonderful picture you've taken until you enlarge it. What looks good small can look outstanding larger. Add a mat and a frame for instant art on your walls. Your favorite photos can mean more to you than commercial ones even if they aren't as professional.

For a good quality enlargement, photo shops can make poster-size prints from your negative or photos. You get the best results when the photo is enlarged from a good negative—the larger the negative, the more detail. The 35mm film negative (measuring 1" x 1 1/2") can make a good quality poster. Blurry focus or using grainy film gives disappointing enlargements. View your negative on a light box through a loupe (magnifying lens) to assess detail and focus. The photo shop can assess what size poster your negative or photo can achieve. Choose anything from a simple frame with no mat to an elegant made-to-size frame lined with one or more mats to feature the photo even more.

Joan Hall's scenic photo was enlarged, double matted, and framed for display.

You need:
- A favorite photo
- Access to a color copier or camera shop
- Frame 20" x 26" (or as needed)
- Mat board and cutter
- Spray mount

1 Choose a sharp-focus photo for your poster, or the enlargement will be blurry. The least expensive way to make a poster is to copy the photo to 11" x 17". Each dimension will double when enlarging a photo 100%. For larger posters, a photocopy set to about 275% makes your photo the maximum 11" x 17" size. Or, since copiers can make up to a 400% enlargement, you can splice two photocopies. The photo shop can make even larger copies with a more complex machine, which will cost more.

2 Mount the photocopy on stiff backing.

3 Select a frame and trim the copy to fit, or cut a mat to fill in the space between the poster and the frame. Double mats, some cut into elaborate shapes, are popular now. Or choose an inexpensive frame that allows for changing the poster scene as you wish.

Sources: Dick Blick catalog, Michaels, Home Goods

Joan and Garrett Hall take turns shooting photos on their mountain climbs. Garrett photographed this scene using their SLR Minolta 5000 I camera with a negative so clear it could be enlarged to 24" x 36" and framed to 34" X 46".

Photo Tip *Taking good pictures*

What do you really see in the viewfinder? Analyze your photos to find out. Is the flower you liked lost somewhere in the distance? Is half of your friend cut off, yet lots of sky shows? Your eye/brain combination is a lot more selective than the camera. You can sort out a scene, but the camera must take what you focus on. Use the viewfinder as a picture frame to analyze the scene for over-all design, for shapes, forms, and colors.

Refocus your mind to view the scene as shadows and highlights, not as Aunt Jane or your dog. Better yet, begin with something that doesn't move, say a flower, to have time to analyze the scene. Does the flower stand out clearly? Are there competing shapes in the background? Is it big enough, or should you move in closer? Does backlighting silhouette the subject?

Give yourself a photography assignment: Shoot for textures in the back yard, aim at neighborhood faces, record area houses, or take shots of food in the kitchen. You'll learn to take better photos and get good photos to use in projects or to hang on the wall.

Photo Art & Craft

Kids' masks

Artist models: Briana and Brent Hood, Ross Hall

Have fun with photography. Plan a photo session of your models—kids or grownups. Pat Hall held the single spotlight in various positions on her children to give exaggerated, single source lighting. Italian painters used this same device (using lamps or candles) for dramatic effects, calling it chiaroscuro. These results aim to be dramatic, but use any full-face photo you like for a mask.

Cutout eye holes allow the wearer to peek out of the mask.

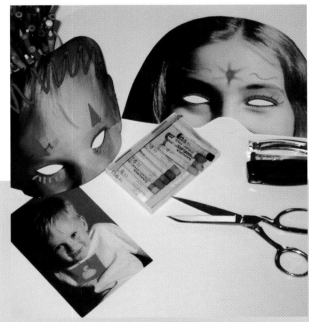

For a fun project, make masks. Take pictures of the kids, photocopy them to face size, color with Cray-Pas oil crayons, add clear laminate, staple on rubber bands, and join the party.

You need:
- Flood light and holder
- Extension cord
- Camera (Olympus 140 zoom used here)
- Oil pastel crayons
- Wax colored pencils (Prismacolor)
- Scissors
- Staple gun
- Rubber bands

1 Take photographs of your kids with dramatic lighting from the side, top, and below with the camera flash turned off. For Halloween masks, encourage them to make funny faces. Some kids won't need any encouragement!

Pat Hall holds a spotlight on Ross to get exaggerated lighting for the mask project.

Ross uses oil crayons to color an enlarged photocopy of his photo to make his mask.

Briana embellishes her mask with cosmetic flair.

2 Photocopy photos so the eyes are 2 1/2" to 3" apart center-to-center, and the face is 8" or 9" across, including ears or hair.

3 Use Cray-Pas® oil pastel crayons or Prismacolor wax pencils to elaborate on the features. Briana enhanced her make-up to video star level, while Ross covered his first copy with black.

Here Briana cuts out Ross' mask, which was laminated to fix the colors and strengthen the paper.

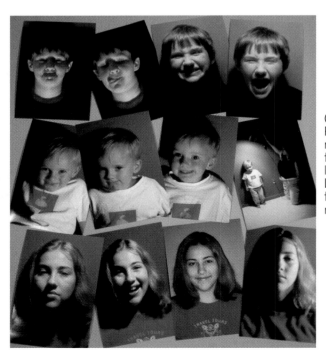

4 When finished, unroll a sheet of adhesive laminating film onto the mask to strengthen the mask and keep the pastels from smearing. Smooth out any air bubbles, and rub to adhere firmly so the colors show clearly.

5 Cut out the eyeholes, making them large enough for good vision. Staple rubber bands at the sides to wrap around the ears, or staple a long band across from side to side. Embellish the mask further by adding feathers, ribbons, fake hair, beads, buttons, or whatever comes to mind for the look you want.

Note: Masks limit vision and should not be worn outside.

Sources: Kinko's, JM Laminate, Michaels, Dick Blick

Grandkids Brent, Ross, and Briana mug as they pose for making Halloween masks. Lighting comes from side angles to make creepy faces.

Photo Art & Craft

How do those movie producers make such scary scenes? Aside from creepy music, it's the dramatic lighting. That's a blank, flat screen up there until the images come on. Suddenly it's three-dimensional, even though you know this is only projected light and shadow. Photography works the same way as eyes do. Light is reflected onto sensitized film or is digitized—no light, no photo.

Look at your album photos to check where the light is falling. Direct overhead sunlight gives shadowed eyes. Light shining directly into faces gets squinty looks with no shadows. Light from behind, called backlighting, silhouettes the darkened subject, as in the lily photo.

Portrait photographers using "available light" often prefer the soft, pink, morning-side lighting or late afternoon, golden lighting. Studio photographers adjust a group of spotlights or floodlights for the effects they want.

To experiment with light and shadows, shoot a roll of black and white film under varying lighting conditions. This forces you to see light and shadow minus beguiling color. Contrast, texture, and design replace color as focus.

Backlighting makes these lilies glow in a way front lighting could not. Try shooting your subject from different lighting angles.

Tell a story

One picture may be worth a thousand words, but a series of them can tell the whole story. Ross thrilled at the way the mirror spun, how one side reflected his image, and how the other magnified it. He was astonished that he could see me there too. I clicked away with a flash camera, aiming downward to simplify the background and avoid glare. These six shots from the series tell the story.

To present them artistically, standard-sized 4" x 6" photographs are mounted on a heavy-weight, art paper. They are placed casually as you might lay them out, not in regimented order. Using a long ruler, a pencil line fenced in the central images. Hand-written words border the images, as much for artistic effect as for message.

A series of shots of Ross Hall tells the story about his discovery of the properties of a shaving mirror.

Simon Layton took a series of car photos at Detroit's yearly Dream Cruise. That smoke is exhaust from one of the classic cars in the parade.

You need:

- Six (or as desired) photographs 4" x 6"
- Finished frame with glass (or plastic) 25" x 30" (or as needed)
- Backing: Poster board 25" x 30"
- Thick art-quality paper 25" x 30"
- Note paper

Supplies:

30" ruler, mat cutter, No. 2 pencil, white glue or double-sided mounting tape, clear tape

1 Select six related photos. Luck often plays a part in people pictures, so choose existing photos and augment them with additional shots or plan on taking a series of photos for this purpose.

2 For the mounting background, use the ruler and mat cutter to cut the art paper and mat board to fit the frame.

3 Arrange the photographs in a block as shown, or put them in a line horizontally, vertically, or as best tells the story. Try various arrangements, casual or neatly aligned. Tape the photos temporarily in place on their backside. With the ruler, pencil in a light bordering line.

4 Hand-write or print your story poem to accompany the photos. Cut the words in strips and lay them out around the photos for fit.

5 Glue printed words in place, or write them on the background, using the strip as a guide.

6 Mount the photographs in place with glue or double mounting tape. Frame the result, add the backing, and wire it to hang.

Sources: Frame kits; Dick Blick for mat board, mat cutter, glue, and tape

Photo Tip   *Series shots*

Still shots can tell a story as well as a movie camera. They stay frozen in time, while the movie whirs on. In this project, grandson Ross discovered his grandfather's shaving mirror. "First times" have an excitement that later staged ones rarely manage, so keep a loaded camera handy at all times. It may save money to take one or two photos at a time, but the chances of getting a terrific photo or a wonderful series are better when you take more. Series ideas include a trip to the market, a special event, nostalgic objects, friends, or family. Or expand your idea to cover elapsed time with seasonal photos of your garden or a yearly picture of a child.

Variations may tell your story better and add interest visually, so try these techniques: Vary the distance by taking close-up, mid-range, and distant shots. Vary the lighting by taking shadowed and bright shots. Vary the perspective by taking front, side, back, overhead, and other shots. Vary the emphasis by focusing on one part of the scene or another.

This series of photos taken at the market shows the value of moving in close for more design-oriented shots.

Using photos and photocopies

Tinting photos

The fashion for coloring classic black and white photos has returned. Before the advent of good, stable color photography, hand colorists gave life to black and white studio portraits with soft-tint pastel colors or transparent oil paint for a more solid overlay. The impermanent pastel colors have gone by the wayside, but archival-quality photographic oils are still available. So, too, are photo dyes. With oils, best results come from sepia or brown-toned photographs on matte papers. Oils allow for mixing colors, lightening dark areas, and for wiping off mistakes. Opaque oils on the photo can appear as an oil painting.

Water-soluble dyes allow for faster results than these time-consuming techniques. Use these dyes to remember realistic colors or to embellish a print creatively. Some TV commercials air in black and white with startling splashes of color these days. This technique toys with the illusion of the scene and creates emphasis. Use extra black-and-white prints to experiment with this lively technique.

Contemporary tinting of old black and white photos aims for emphasis rather than realism.

For dye-coloring you need:
- Photo
- Watercolor pens or dyes
- Small brushes
- Dye remover pen or solution
- Sponge
- Kodak Photo-Flow
- Pan of water

For photo-oil coloring you need:
- Photo-transparent oils in tubes and pencils
- Cotton balls and swabs
- Vinyl eraser
- Palette or plate for mixing colors
- Drafting tape and finishing spray
- Matte-finish photo

layers to intensify colors. Wash out mistakes immediately with the dye remover pen, or soak the whole print for one or two hours.

Photo-oil coloring method

1 If possible have the photo sepia-toned to soften and brown-tint the shadows. Use a matte-finish photo, or coat a glossy surface with pre-color spray. Oil tinting works best on larger portraits, since most other photographs have too much landscape detail. Use removable drafting tape to affix the print to a flat surface.

2 Use cotton swabs to apply a thin layer of color. First coat large areas with a base color, such as flesh tone, and blend deeper tones into this. Create highlights by swabbing away or erasing color. Use darker tones in the shadows. Detail small areas, such as eyebrows and lips, with the wax pencils. Mistakes can be wiped off to start over. Aim for well blended, minimal coverage.

3 Let the photo dry three days in a dust-free box, then coat with a finishing spray to stabilize the colors.

Dye-coloring method

1 Use a black and white photo in RC, or fiber-based paper in glossy or matte finish. Choose a photo with minimal detail for easiest working. Lacking this, have your color negative printed in black and white. Close-up shots or large-sized photos will be easiest to work on.

2 Moisten the print with Kodak Photo-Flow or Dawn Free using 1 teaspoon per quart of water in a pan. Keep the photo moist with this solution while you work by applying it with a sponge or brush. Experiment on a scrap photo using light pressure. Dilute to apply the color smoothly, and then build up

Sources: Spotpen, Inc.™; Kodak Photo-Flow®; Eagle® sable brushes; Dick Blick; Michaels

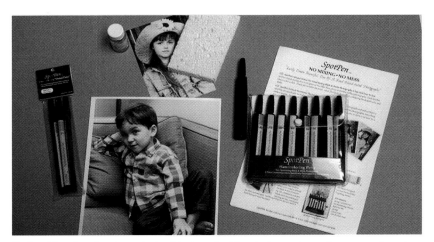

Tinting kits allow for dye-coloring black and white photographs as they were done in the days before color photography.

Scenic coasters

If you have a hobby such as gardening, you can display your flower photos year round by making coasters or tiles from a collection of them. For these, standard 4" x 6" photographs were trimmed to fit a wooden form or a 4" tile. You could make your own backing of wood, plastic, or ceramic. The photos are adhered directly and then varnished to protect and waterproof the image surface. On one, a sheer fabric was glued on, muting the colors. With backing, these can be used as coasters but not as trivets for hot dishes. For a different effect, use colored tiles and cut out the imagery before gluing it on.

To make coasters, collect a series of photos, wooden blocks for backing, and glue. Varnish the surface for protection.

You need:
- Six photographs 4" x 6"
- Six wooden blocks 3" x 4" or six tiles 4"
- Backing: Felt 8" x 10"
- Optional: Sheer fabric
- One piece of template paper 6" x 6"

Supplies:
Scissors, grease pencil, sandpaper, acrylic paint and brush, decoupage glue, sponge, water-based polyurethane, paintbrush

Glue the block on the back of the your photo, and trim away the extra.

Photo Art & Craft

1 Select a related collection of favorite photographs.

2 Make a template (pattern) by tracing the block on thick paper and cutting out this window.

3 Place the window over the photograph to select the best part of the design. Trace the window with grease pencil and trim it with scissors outside this line, then rub off the pencil marks. Repeat to select images from all the photos.

4 Dilute the glue to cream. Paint or squeegee the glue onto the back of the photo. Press the photo onto the block or tile, and roll the glue bottle across it to push out all air bubbles. Trim the photo edges to match the block or tile edges. Wipe off glue with a damp sponge and let it dry.

5 Photos printed from modern films are color intensified, and sometimes just too bright. To soften the effect, glue on a fine fabric in ecru or tan over the photo, using white glue, which dries waterproof and clear.

6 Photo finishes are fairly tough, but for added protection, varnish the surface with spray-on polyurethane. Brushing this on may leave brush marks. For coasters, trace the template on felt, paint the block's reverse side with glue, press on the felt square, and roll to adhere. Trim the edges neatly and let dry.

Sources: Michaels, Hancock Fabrics, or Jo-Ann®

Use favorite scenes like these from Florida to make coasters that remind you of good times.

Labels and tiles

Photos can be better than printed labels for identification. After all, alphabet letters were developed from pictographs (symbolic drawings of real things). This technique of identification can be used in a variety of ways—for contents of drawers, for key racks, coat hangers, treasure boxes, or for family growing markers up the wall.

Pull open the drawer, arrange the stuff inside, and shoot a photo. Then stick it to the front of the drawer for identifying the contents.

You need:

- Photos of people or contents
- A board, cupboard, or box for mounting onto
- Mounting glue or adherent
- Scissors or paper cutter
- JM Laminate

In his photography class, Simon Layton popped in a 3 1/4" square photo of his first car for a CD cover.

1 You may have enough photos on hand. If not, make a list and take the ones you need. Open a drawer, artfully arrange the contents (or a representative few objects) on a flat plane, and photograph them.

2 Trim the photos to size in whatever shape suits your design and space. For a CD label, tuck the photo into the case lid.

3 Align the photos in place, and permanently glue them on with white glue, or use a removable adherent to change the photos as needed. UHU® HoldIt® is a removable plastic adhesive that can be reused. It is clean and won't dry out.

4 For tiles, use white glue to permanently adhere photos. Laminate the photo for protection.

Sources: Kodak film, UHU HoldIt, JM Laminate

Glue photos on tiles to decorate your kitchen.

Photo Tip 6 — *Depth of field*

Quick cameras with a fixed focus cannot focus on objects closer than two feet or so. For close-ups, you need a variable focus camera or an auxiliary macro lens to take objects as close as a few inches in sharp detail. Some point-and-shoot cameras, such as the Olympus 140 zoom that I use, let you know with flashing lights if you get too close to focus on the scene. The larger SLR (single lens reflex) cameras show you the scene through the lens, so you know if it's in focus. Both cameras tell you if there is insufficient light.

Close-up shots will have a narrow depth of field. This means the object in the center of the photo, where the camera focuses, will be sharp but objects not on the same plane (distance from the camera) will be blurry. Have you ever taken a close-up photo of two friends where the center background was sharp, but the friends on each side were blurred? That shows depth of field. Make sure that what you need in focus is the same distance from the camera as the center of focus area. On auto focus cameras, you can override this by center-focusing on the object—keep your finger on the button to maintain focus, move to frame the scene, then click. On very close-up shots, the depth of field is even less. A heaped pile of threads will show some in focus, some not. Spread them out on a flat surface and aim straight on, and all will be in focus. To increase depth of field, close down the F stop to the smallest aperture with longer time.

This scene from the Sarasota game (project #22) shows a short depth-of-field with a limited area in focus, the rest blurred.

Home decor

35

37

40

42

44

46

48

50

These place mats feature scenes taken in the back yard of a Florida home.

Easy place mats

My assignment: Shoot close-up pictures in the yard to show each plant in detail, even to places where bugs chewed the leaves. This means getting close enough to eliminate other extraneous visuals. For this you need a camera with a close-up or zoom lens (see Photo tip on page 99). Take more scenes than you plan to use, in case of bugs, etc.

Use any imagery you wish for a place mat, such as your cottage and a map of how to get there, your child with a hand-drawn picture, a picture from the newspaper and accompanying article, or a cluster of photos from an event. Remember that a plate of food will be sitting in the middle of your place mat, so aim for texture more than scene in your photo. Or tack the place mat on the bulletin board.

The series of 4" x 6" photos on the left were photocopied to large size and laminated to make place mats.

You need:
- 6 photo scenes
- Double laminating sheets 11 1/4" x 17 1/4"

1 Take a series of related photos, featuring over-all texture or a bordering scene. Select the best six. Further, do two series of shots and make your place mats double sided.

2 Color-photocopy the photos at a local printing or office store. First, copy one photo as an example. If the color reproduction is poor or there are white lines across it, the machine is not in good working order. Ask for a better

machine, or go to another store. Copy all six photos to 11" x 17", the maximum size for most machines.

3 The office store can double-laminate them by sliding the copy (or two, back to back) into the double laminate sheet and running it through the heat-sealing machine. Lacking this, use craft-store laminate in 9" x 12" sheets. This material sticks by adhesive, not heat. Begin at one

end, carefully removing the backing and rolling the laminate onto the copy. Make no mistakes; it is stuck forever. Add more laminate if needed to cover. Roll laminate on the reverse side.

4 Trim the edges as needed.

Sources: Office Depot®, Kinko's, Xerox, Canon®, JM Laminating sheets

Individualized place mats add to a creative table display.

To make quick place mats for inventive décor, have photocopies laminated at the office supply store.

Photo Art & Craft

Eat your vegetables, or at least enjoy looking at them.

Decoupage plates

Friends joke that I plan the table decoration for a dinner party, then decide the right color of food. It's true; I love dishes and delight in seeing new patterns on the table. I'll begin with any component—the tablecloth, place mats, napkins, flowers, or dishes. Then I choose the others for effect—casual, bright, whimsical, austere, festive, or formal. You can make your own dish patterns to suit your plan quite easily. The scenes for these inexpensive, glass plates were shot at the Saturday morning market, where stall owners display their foods in mouth-watering glory.

The enlarged images are glued on the reverse side of clear, glass plates and coated with decoupage glue to waterproof them. Do not stack wet plates or wash the decoupage plates in the dishwasher. They must be hand washed, or the paper may loosen. If this happens, don't despair. You can re-glue tiny loose spots. More than tiny damage? Soak the plates in hot water for as long as it takes to remove the image and varnish, then redo them with another set of images.

You need:
- 6 or 8 photos with related theme
- 6 or 8 clear 8" luncheon plates or 10" dinner plates

Supplies and tools:
Decoupage glue, compass for circle, pencil, heavy paper for guide, scissors, acrylic paint, paintbrush, sponge, Prismacolor® pencils to retouch, bowl of water

1 Select or create a series of related photographs. The theme might be market foods, flowers, local scenes, family faces, toys, pets, vacation scenes, or whatever makes an appetizing grouping.

2 Measure across the flat bottom of the plate. Luncheon plates measure about 5" with an outer rim diameter of 8", a dinner plate measures about 7 1/2" with a diameter of 10 3/4". Make the photocopies large enough to cover the bottom of the plate.

Measure the plate base to make a template for your photographs.

3 On heavy paper, draw a circle the diameter of the plate bottom and cut it out. Move this frame over the photocopy to find the best scene.

Adjust the template on the photocopy to select the best part of the image for your plate.

4 Trace the circle, and cut out the image. Or cut out parts of the photocopy and arrange them into a new design. Repeat for all plates.

Carefully cut out the circle for the base of the plate.

5 Use diluted decoupage glue to coat the face side of the image past the edges. Position the image on the plate bottom and rub firmly until the design adheres. Use the glue bottle as a rolling pin until ALL air bubbles disappear and extra glue is squeezed out. (Audrey Busse demonstrates making the plates.)

Brush a coating of diluted decoupage glue onto the photocopy.

6 Clean off any glue with a damp sponge and let dry.

Another way to transfer photos to plates involves soaking the backing paper off the photocopies.

7 For a transparent effect, soak the paper and rub it off, leaving the image imbedded in the glue.

Once the photocopy paper back is saturated, rub it off by hand or sponge.

8 When dry, paint the back of the image. Then coat it with decoupage medium, going over the edge 1/4" onto the plate to seal it.

The decoupage glue traps the photocopy colors, which appear translucent when the paper backing is rubbed off.

Photo Art & Craft

9 Or paint the back of the plate with Royal Coat crackle medium, which will crackle as it dries. Apply a coating of a metallic or contrasting color paint to fill in the cracks. Coat the entire back of the plate with decoupage medium and let dry (not shown).

After the glued-on photocopy has dried, use acrylic paint or decoupage glue to waterproof the back side.

Sources: Michaels, Kinko's, Office Max, Office Depot, Apple Barrel craft paint, Rub and Buff metallic paint, plates from Bed Bath and Beyond®

Scenes taken at the market make succulent imagery when decoupaged onto these glass plates.

Flowered apron

The photo-transfer technique applies a photographic image to fabric without sewing. You can cut out photos or even combine more than one. The finished surface will feel stiffer than plain fabric and will repel water. It can be washed with care. In craft stores, the transfer gel is called transfer medium for fabric, the same substance used to extend acrylic paint (called gel medium).

The photo must be photocopied, since photo emulsion will not release from the backing paper. Remember that the transferred image will appear in reverse, so if this matters or lettering is included have the photocopy reversed or use the face-up technique described on the medium bottle.

This technique works on other surfaces such as a glass plate, ceramic tile, canvas, or any surface on which the gel medium will form a strong bond. It works best on fabric, since you can push the gel print into the fibers. Some reproduction paintings are done this way with simulated brush strokes giving the "original" effect.

Use the photo-transfer technique to add a scene to your apron, shirt, or other fabric.

You need:

- Transfer gel
- Photo
- Apron
- Acrylic paint
- Permanent black marker

Supplies:

Sponge, paintbrush or stiff card to squeegee, bowl of water, scissors, ruler, pencil, stiff foam piece larger than the image

Dimensions:

About 10" x 14"

1 Copy your photo imagery to 11" x 17". The cutout image shown has drawn and painted touches added.

To transfer a photo, first choose the image and trim it to the shape you want.

2 Use a ready-made apron or make your own. Use 2" pins to anchor the apron smooth and taut to a stiff backing covered with freezer paper. With small pencil marks, indicate where to apply the photo-transfer.

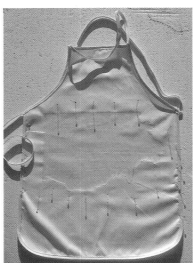

Stretch the fabric apron smooth on a flat surface (foamboard), and pin it.

3 Use a paintbrush or squeegee to apply a thick, even coating of gel to the front of the photocopy. Place it face down on the placement marks.

4 Cover with a paper towel. Roll a glue bottle over the paper towel to flatten out all bubbles and press the gel firmly into the fibers. The image must be totally and firmly glued to the fabric to transfer. Prick any air bubbles with a pin.

5 Remove the towel, and wash off any glue that is on the image backing paper.

6 Let this dry 24 hours.

7 Use a sponge to soak the copy backing. Then peel off as much paper as possible. Rub the remaining paper fibers off with a damp sponge. Keep rubbing until all paper is removed. The image will brighten.

After 24 hours, dampen the photocopy backing paper and rub it all off.

8 If the copy didn't adhere or you rubbed off a few spots, use the acrylic paint for touch up.

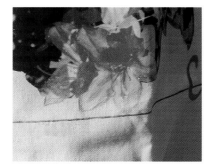

If the photo needs touch up, use acrylic artist colors to paint in the areas.

9 Add lines, lettering, or additional touches using waterproof paint or marker.

10 Coat the image with transfer gel and let dry. Remove the apron from the backing, and you're done.

Sources: Michaels, Hancock Fabrics for apron

Some of the touches you could add to a transferred photo include your signature or a permanent-marker line to frame the photo.

Book tote

Photocopy on fabric

You can promote your book, school or club, kids, or whatever you want.

Transferring imagery to fabric by transfer gel or by the photosensitive emulsion process is a multi-step process. The photocopy machine or computer printer has simplified this. At the ASSI convention, the demonstrators in the Hewlett Packard booth popped my book into their machine, and out came a color print—not in reverse—on a white 8 1/2" x 11" piece of fabric with a clear plastic backing. This printable Photo-To-Fabric® paper (or other brands), comes in 8 1/2" x 11" packages commercially, or you can make your own. If you decide to try making your own, your copy machine must be able to take heavy paper.

You need:
- Photo for imagery
- Ready-made tote bag, or denim 15" x 36" and 1 yard of woven strap 1" wide
- Color photocopier or printer
- Photo-To-Fabric paper

Supplies:
Green embroidery thread, white sewing thread, sewing machine or serger, Heat'n-Bond fusible tape

Dimensions:
14" x 16"

Some newer photocopy machines can copy your photo on fabric.

1 Select an appropriate scene for your tote bag.

2 Photocopy the image to size on the printable fabric.

3 **To prepare your own fabric:** Select a tightly woven, poly-cotton fabric (200 count is best), iron it on freezer paper, trim the edges to 8 1/2" x 11", and run it through a color copy machine or your computer printer. Be sure the printer uses permanent ink. If not, stabilize the colors with a product called Retayne™.

4 If you use a ready-made tote, unstitch one side so you can appliqué the print on while flat. Or make your own tote.

5 Iron Heatn'Bond® fuser on the reverse side of the fabric print. Spread the bag flat, place the print on it, and press to fuse the print to the bag.

6 Using a sewing machine, straight stitch the print in place. Add satin stitching to frame it. Re-sew the bag to finish.

_____

Sources: Hewlett Packard® printer, Hancock Fabrics, Heatn'Bond, Michaels for tote, Sulky® threads

The photocopy was printed in color on fabric backed with a removable plastic film. You can try making your own fabric transfer paper if your copier can accept heavy paper.

Appliqué the photocopy in satin stitching along the edges, and then re-sew the tote.

Shell box

"It looks like wall paper," granddaughter Briana said. This kind of over-all design with no central focus works well when photocopied for covering a box, frame, or other object. The photo shown has a cluster of shells and gemstones. A real shell was added to create a decorative effect. If you use scenic imagery, be sure it is right side up with sky for the top surface. Or get creative and collage the box with cutouts.

You need:

- Photograph
- Wooden box 4" x 4" x 5"
- Decoupage glue
- Foam brush
- Dish of water
- Scissors
- Shells
- Paper for pattern
- Razor blade
- Polyurethane coating

To cover a wooden box, assemble your supplies and tools.

1 A photo with an over-all design such as shells, clouds, or a party crowd works best. Photocopy it to 11" x 17". Make two copies to piece the design if necessary.

2 Measure the box and make a paper pattern. For the top add 1/2" on each side to fold over the edges. Cut the four sides in one long strip, plus 1/2" at one end, keeping the imagery right side up.

3 Remove the box top handle. Place the photocopy, evenly coated with diluted glue, on the box top. Roll or rub firmly to remove ALL air bubbles.

4 With the box lid on, glue the side strip and wrap it around the box. Rub firmly to adhere and remove all air bubbles.

5 Press in slightly at the lid/box joining to score.

When the glue dries, cut at the joining with a razor blade to open the box.

6 Coat the entire box with polyurethane. Screw the knob back on the top, and glue on an assortment of shells or whatever relates to your photo.

Sources: Office Max, Office Depot, Kinko's, Michaels

Measure the box top and sides, then cut these pieces from the photocopy to glue on.

Use decoupage or white glue to stick the photocopy on the box sides. Be sure to rub out all air bubbles to a smooth finish.

A photo of a cluster of shells on a vendor's table, photographed at close range, gives an over-all design.

Cloud lamp

If you've ever tried to cover a lampshade, you'll be happy to know one comes covered with adhesive to roll on a photocopy or fabric. Also, there's a sticky wooden base for photographs, photocopies, or fabric as well. Here, the base shows a pond scene, so the shade needed related imagery, which required two days of running outside to photograph clouds at different times of the day.

Other factors affect your choice of scene. Incandescent bulbs cast a warm, yellow color through the shade, which changes shade colors. Also consider how the imagery matches at the joinings. A scene with a base line will not easily fit onto the semi-circular shade pattern unless you do a lot of piecing. For a border effect, you could cut out individual elements and decoupage them on. If these admonitions constrict your idea too much, ignore them and do it your way.

Cover a lampshade and base with scenes to enhance your decor, such as these fluffy clouds.

Warm light from the incandescent bulb will glow through the photocopy.

You need:
- Plain lampshade
- Photocopy of imagery

Supplies and tools:
Spray glue (or a lampshade and base with an adhesive surface), large paper for pattern (newsprint), scissors, pencil, razor blade to trim

1 A photo with an over-all pattern works best.

2 For the lamp, some craft stores carry shades and bases with adhesive surfaces and a paper pattern for cutting out the applied imagery. Lacking this, fit paper onto the lampshade, and tape the overlapping edges to temporarily hold it in place.

3 Trace along the shade top and lower edges, mark the overlap vertically, and cut out the pattern. Leave 1/4" extra along all edges to be trimmed to fit later. Repeat for the base pattern.

Make a pattern of your lampshade and have your photographs photocopied to 11" x 17".

4 Make two or more photo-copies (11" x 17") to fit the shade pattern. Adjust the copy over the pattern for the best placement. Then trace it. Cut out one piece first, adjust the joining to the second image, trace and cut out the second piece.

Cut out half of the shade pattern, or all that will fit on the photocopy.

5 You must place the image on correctly the first try. Hold the copy away from the lamp. Align the vertical joining with the shade seam and

Carefully roll the cloud print onto the adhesive shade.

carefully roll the copy in place. Press out any air bubbles.

6 Apply the second shade section, and glue the overlapping joints. Trim the photocopy edges using a sharp utility knife, razor blade, or scissors.

7 If you wish, embellish the edge with tape or ribbon.

8 For the base, varnish or paint the exposed parts with the color you want and let dry.

9 Photocopy your photo, make a pattern to fit, and apply the photocopy as directed. Glue the overlapping joint.

Sources: Michaels, Jo-Ann, Kinko's, Office Max, Office Depot

Place cards

These versatile cards serve as invitations, place cards, and thank-you notes all for the same party. For the invitation, fill in the party information by hand or computer, address the envelopes, and send to the guests. For place cards, print or write the names, fold the cards in half horizontally, and arrange them on the table. After the party, use the cards to write thank-you notes to partygoers.

The card is designed to use standard paper and envelope sizes available in office supply stores. It can be constructed three ways. One, order duplicate copies of the photograph, card stock, and paper, then paste up each individually. Two, design one master card, and photocopy the number of invitations, place cards, and thank-you notes you'll need. Or three, scan the photo into your computer, set up the card for each use, and print it out.

With one design you can make versatile cards for a birthday party or other event.

For quick place cards, fold a 4" square of colored, heavy paper in half, stick on a large gold seal, and glue on the cut-out face.

You need:

- One picture of the birthday person
- Green decorative paper 4" x 5 1/2"
- Ivory paper 2 3/4" x 4 3/4"
- 12 ready-made envelopes 4 3/8" x 5 3/4"
- Glue stick
- Scissors
- Black pen

Optional: Use 18 copies of the photo, 5 sheets of 8" x 11" green decorative paper or card stock, and 3 sheets ivory paper.

1 Use a full-head photo with good lighting. If you want to save the original, make a photocopy. Cut out the head, leaving a thin outline of background. Heads look odd if trimmed too closely.

2 To make the place cards and invitations, cut the decorative paper into four equal pieces, 4 1/4" x 5 1/2".

3 On the ivory page, use a heavy pen to mark six rectangles, each 2 3/4" x 4 3/4". Cut outside these outlines for a dark border.

4 Glue the ivory block vertically on the green card. Glue the head below the centerline. Embellish with watercolors or oil crayons, as you wish.

5 Type or hand-letter your message on the ivory rectangle. Do this after the cards are photocopied, or by computer before cutting out the rectangles (if the cards are individual paste-ups).

Fill in the open area with party information, by hand or by computer, to make the invitations.

6 For thank-you notes, change the ivory message, paste it on, and print copies. For a double-fold card, photocopy the thank-you card in the lower

With the same format, you can write thank-you notes in the open area.

right corner of an 8 1/2" x 11" page and fold in the center horizontally, then fold vertically.

7 Print blank copies for the place cards, and then hand-letter.

Sources: Wausau Papers® Astro Bright® fluorescent envelopes or Columbian® envelopes Westvaco® division to fit folded 8 1/2" x 11" paper; Provo Craft and Novelty® scrap pads, paper available at Office Depot, Office Max, Kmart®, Michaels, etc.

For place cards, fold the plain cards horizontally, so the honoree's face shows. Write in the guest's name.

Champagne celebration

Wine or food is nearly always an appropriate hostess gift. Choose a magnum of champagne—it has room for a larger photo—and make a personal label. This label shows us with good friends Jim and Helen Balmer on their 40th anniversary cruise. It now celebrates their 50th Anniversary with congratulations printed across the top and below the photos. This idea need not be limited to wine or drinkables. Make a label for any bottle, can, or box.

How about your child who always wanted to star on the Wheaties or Corn Flakes box? Or perhaps special labels for your canned goods, a picture of your special tomato plant on the salsa jar, or the string bean pole on the bean jar? Use a photo, scissors, and photocopier; or use a scanner and computer to make these personal labels.

You need:
- Photo
- Bottle
- Text (by word processor program)
- JM Laminate

Supplies:
Clear tape, scissors or paper cutter, ruler

Begin with a magnum of champagne, a picture of the honorees, and the text you want to include for a personalized label.

1 Select an event-related photo (4" x 6") of an anniversary, birthday, promotion, retirement, or even special food. Write the label message using as few words as possible. Who reads long labels (except for dietary info)? The font here is a graceful one called BankenScript.

2 Print or draw the text and add hand-drawn embellishments on white paper. To paste up, trim the strips of text to size with a paper cutter or scissors and ruler. Then tape them around the photo.

3 Color-photocopy the paste-up to the size of label you want. Return your photo back to its album.

4 Cover the label with a laminate sheet for extra protection from moisture or handling. Trim the label to size, and glue or clear tape the label on the bottle—perhaps on the back—so the manufacturer's label can identify the contents, if needed.

5 Tie a decorative ribbon around the neck and present to the honorees.

Sources: BankenScript by Expresiv Fonts, part of the Ornate Font Collection (World Art)

Computers have elegant and graceful fonts to make your label. Lacking this, you can hand-letter calligraphy, and add whatever details you like.

Chapter Three

Making toys

53

55

58

60

62

64

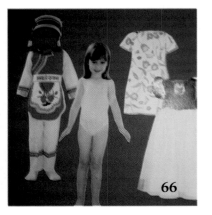

66

Displayed on a table, boy blocks make your child your favorite work of art.

Boy blocks

A chance photo of son Garrett, looking stiffly military, provided imagery for this idea. He later donned the same outfit and assumed the same pose for photos from five more angles (right side, left side, rear, top, and bottom). For each shot, you need to stay the same distance from the subject, unless you can manipulate the image size by darkroom, computer, or copier.

The blocks can be made from various materials: Hardboard or Masonite (a pressed fiber board from 3/8" to 1/4" thick), model wood (a clear 1/4" thick wood), foam board (a polystyrene foam core laminated with white coated paper stock), or a combination of these materials. Photos on every side of the block create a three-dimensional reality. The six identical blocks allow for arranging the boy to do a variety of tricks—stand on his head, span two boy-blocks, and other acrobatic poses.

You need:
- 6 photo views of the subject, one from each angle
- Enlarger, photocopier, or scanner and printer
- 1/4" foam board or hardboard 15" x 20"
- Mat board

Supplies and tools:
Sandpaper, saw or utility knife, ruler, glue, brads, razor blade, Aleene's™ Tacky Glue, JM Laminate sheet

1 Against a plain background, take shots of the model from all six views. Mark the spot for model and camera to ensure consistent size. Shoot down from a stepladder for the top of the head and bottoms of the feet (soles upward).

2 Enlarge your photos to size.

3 The box shown is 3" x 4 1/2" x 14". For sturdy boxes, use 1/4" plywood, 3/8" Masonite or a combination of the two. For lightweight boxes, use 1/4" foam board.

4 Measure and cut accurately. Cut the front and back pieces as needed for your photo: Cut two sidepieces the same size as the front and back pieces, minus the thickness of the front and back pieces. Cut the top and bottom pieces, minus two thicknesses of the front and side pieces.

5 Assemble the box with precise corners for smooth sides. On hard materials, glue the sides together and nail with countersunk brads. Fill in the holes and sand smooth. On foam board, glue mat board over the side and top pieces for smooth sides and neat corners.

6 To adhere the photo, use diluted white glue and rub the photo firmly. Trim the edges exactly straight with a sharp utility blade. Continue to glue on and trim the rest of the photos.

7 For foam board and jet-printer copy, cover the entire finished box with laminate to stabilize and waterproof.

Sources: The Home Depot®, Kinko's, Jo-Ann, Hancock

Photograph the model from six views for the blocks—front, back, right and left sides, top and bottom. The blocks can be posed endlessly with the boy standing on his head, stacked at angles, or doing other tricks.

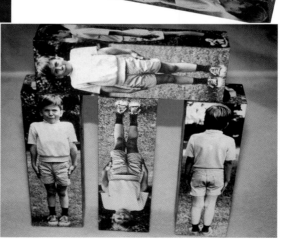

Photo Art & Craft

Jumping Jill

Example by Claudia Hall Stroud

Here's a charming action toy design that has been around for ages. Pull the string and the jumping jack jumps. This toy requires advance planning to pose the model. Make this figure small for an ornament or large for a toy. Use thin mat board for easy cutting or thicker wood for longer wear. The legs and arms attach to the body with screws or pins. To mechanize the toy, join a harness to the arms and legs. Tie strings to the arm and leg tops, and join the strings to make a pull cord.

You need:
- Two photographs of the model
- Stiff backing material 9" x 15": Masonite, foam board, mat board, thin plastic, or thick aluminum foil
- Harness: Cord or monofilament line and bead

Supplies and tools:
Tracing paper, pencil, circle guide, glue, needle or nail, sharp utility knife or jig saw, screwdriver

Dimensions:
14" x 14"

1 Photograph the model using floor marks for both model and camera to keep the image size the same. For pose No.1, take the model fully dressed. Hold the skirt out to the sides to cover leg movement. For pose No.2, photograph the model wearing only body-hugging clothing with legs apart and arms out.

This jumping-jill toy requires two poses of the model.

2 Print the images in a darkroom or photocopy them to size. The figure shown is 14" tall—the body section is 8" x 7", each leg is 9" x 2", and each arm is 7" x 1 1/4".

3 For a paper pattern, trace both full figures.

4 On pose No. 1, cut out the torso and head, minus the limbs. On the reverse side, mark a dot at the shoulder and hip joints, 1/2" from the body edge (or as suits the size of your toy).

5 On pose No. 2, to round the limb-top ends, draw a 1" circle at the shoulder on each arm. Draw a 1" circle at the hip end of each leg. Mark a center hole on these rounded limb ends, and cut out the arms and legs.

6 On the rounded end of each limb, mark a harness dot 1/8" from the top edge in the center.

7 Align the No. 1 and No. 2 dots with pins to rotate the shoulder or hip joints, and see how your figure moves. Adjust the No. 1 dots as needed.

8 Trace the pattern pieces on the photos, cut out, and glue each piece on stiff backing.

9 Cut out these pieces using a jig saw for Masonite, a utility knife for mat board, or heavy scissors for a plastic sheet or heavy foil. If some parts—fingers, toes, or hair—are too narrow, cut out around them.

10 Punch or drill the holes: For Masonite or plywood, drill screw holes for joints partway into pose No. 1 (so screws do not pierce the front photo). On pose No. 2, drill all the way through the joints for the arms and legs.

On thinner backings, joined with fasteners (a round brass head with two prongs that open), punch a hole all the way through the dot marks for the joints.

Before attaching arms and legs, drill or punch the small harness marks and attach a cord to the harness holes.

Drill a small hole at the top of the head, 18" from the edge.

11 **To assemble:** On thick backing, insert 1/2" screws from the back through the arms and legs, and screw into the reverse side of the body (pose No.1). On the thinner backing, use paper fasten-

Cut out the arms and legs with rounded tops, and join them to the body with small screws, so they rotate.

ers, or sew a bead on each side, joined by a strong thread.

12 **To make the harness:** Tie on the head cord. On the reverse side, with arms and legs hanging down, tie the arm cords together in the cen-ter. Tie the leg cords together in the center. Tie the arm and leg cords together at the leg knot. Braid all four cords, thread on a bead, and tie a knot. Hold the head string, and pull on the braid to make the figure jump.

Sources: The Home Depot for lumber and tools, Office Depot or Office Max for paper fasten-ers, art store or Michaels for glue

This jumping jack is made from heavy painted aluminum foil with beads on thread for the joint fasteners.

String a harness as shown to make the Jack or Jill jump.

Little people

If you love to cluster a group of family photos, here's a way to make a favorite shot really stand out. Mount it on a sturdy surface such as 1/4" plastic, foam core, or wood. Then cut it out and stand it on a base. For this project, you need to take or select a photo that shows the entire person, animal, house, trophy, or whatever. It's also best if the photo is well lit, with no heavy shadows, on a light background.

A photo shop in our town called Seeger People specializes in photo figures, shooting single figures and groups with perfect focus and ideal flood lighting. Their photos are backed by white plastic which requires a saw to cut out. Model wood (clear ash) and a jig or coping saw will work for your projects.

You need:

- Photo 4" x 6"
- 1/4" clear wood panel, plastic, or foam board 4" x 9"
- Tacky Glue or decoupage glue

Supplies and tools:

Jig saw, coping saw or band saw with narrow blade, varnish or paint, file or sandpaper

Dimensions:

About 2 1/2" x 5" x 1/4", plus the base

Favorite pictures of little people really stand out among family pictures when they are mounted on a stiff backing and cut out.

1 Use a complete figure photo, taken in good lighting, with a simple outline. Tiny fingers are difficult to cut around.

2 Glue the photo to a background material—plastic, wood, or foam board—using Tacky Glue or decoupage glue. Rub firmly to completely adhere the glue. Let dry.

3 Use a jigsaw, band saw, or coping saw with a narrow or round blade to cut around the figure, skipping sharp inside corners (at the neck, for example). Then make two cuts into these sharp corners.

4 Smooth the edges with a file or sandpaper, but don't mar the photo surface.

5 For a base, cut out a piece of wood or plastic, about 2" x 3" or as fits. Smooth the edges. Varnish or paint it an appropriate color.

6 Glue the figure to the base, or use tiny screws to join.

_____

Sources: Wood from Michaels, The Home Depot, or miniatures stores

The relative size of these cutouts of Bradley and Hattie Stroud as small children is quite clear compared to the family cat, Comet.

Sarasota scenes

Game board

If you have a favorite place where you like to vacation, you can make a game of it. Sort through your photos for a related collection, plan to shoot a series on your next trip, or stay home and photograph your house, yard, neighborhood, and town. Arrange the photos into an aerial map, and make up a game.

To make a game like the Sarasota scenes, assemble 18 photographs, overlay a dotted game path, and laminate them together.

You need:
- 18 scenic photos 3" x 5" or 4" x 6"
- 4 to 6 people photos
- Mat board 24" x 24"
- Stickers 3/4"
- Colored printer paper
- Wood or stiff mat board 1/4" thick
- Polyclay or wood cubes

Supplies
Mounting glue, laminate sheets, scissors

1 Collect 18 or more related horizontal photos to give choice in layout. Lay out the photos in a grid, three across and six high, creating a cohesive scene. If your photos are a mix of horizontal and vertical, fit them together like a puzzle, trimming where needed.

2 Cut the mat board into two pieces, 12" x 24", so the game board can fold in the center.

3 Fix the photos on the mat board with glue or double-sided tape. Or you can photocopy the result and return your photos to their album before the next step.

4 Plan the path of the game. Print the names of places, making up instructions such as "go back two" or "proceed to–." Print the instructions on colored paper by computer or by hand.

5 Cut out each game space, and lay out the path of round stickers and instruction game spaces. Then stick them on.

6 For glued-down photos, cover the game with laminate sheets to create a smooth, sturdy playing surface. For a photocopy, laminate or glue the copies to mat board. Tape the center fold on the back.

7 Select four to six full-length photos of people in playful, frontal poses for game pieces. Photocopy the players to 2" or 3" tall. Glue them on 1/4" board or stiff mat board, and cut them out. Make bases of buttons, polymer clay, or wood, and glue on the figures.

That's Michael Goodrich's game piece hopping along the path of stickers.

8 Add a die (dice) to play.

———

Sources: Kinko's, office store, JM Laminate from Michaels, Jo-Ann for buttons

Ross Hall reaches across the board to move his game piece (a sturdy photo of one of his cousins), as he and Pat Hall play the Sarasota scenes.

Jessie cat pull toy

You can turn the family cat into a pull toy.

Here's a way to keep a beloved pet around forever. Choose a picture of the pet from your collection, or catch the subject in a compact pose. Easier said than done. Best to keep your camera loaded, and snap off a shot when your pet hits a good pose. Move slowly, or you'll scare the pet away. Once you've got a good shot, enlarge it, glue it on a wooden backing, and cut out the image. Use toy parts to make wheels and add a pull cord.

This project works with photos of people, too. Pose the subject sitting or lying down, compactly posed.

You need:

- Photo of pet or person in a compact pose
- Backing: 1" wooden board 8" x 12" or as needed
- Base: 1" board 3" x 12"
- Four wheels
- Four axle pins
- Pull cord 12" to 30" as needed
- Sheet of laminate
- Eight 1" square mat board pieces

Tools and Supplies:

Drill and bit, jig saw (Sears Craftsman), acrylic paint, paintbrush, wooden bead, screws

Photo Art & Craft

1 Select a photo of the sub-ject with a flat base line, compact enough to saw out. Make a copy of the photo, en-larging it to 8" x 12". Make a second copy in reverse for the backside.

2 Roll laminate carefully onto the photos. The laminate will not peel off without taking the surface with it. Glue the photo onto the board and smooth down firmly.

3 Using a jigsaw, band saw, or hand coping saw, cut out the figure with an 1/8" outside the outline. Align the reversed photo, so that it fits exactly, and glue it on the back. Trim the edges.

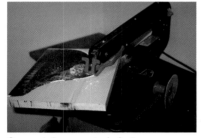
Saw out the mounted photo.

4 Cut out the wooden base, and sand the cut edges. Mark a centerline on the base bottom and drill screw holes 2" from each end.

Screw up into the backing board to join these pieces.

5 Paint the cut edges black. Paint the entire base, and decorate it with color. Paint or varnish the wheels and axle in a contrasting color. Screw the base to the cutout figure.

Decorate the pull toy as you wish.

6 Mark and drill axle holes, two on each side of the base, 2" from each end. Fill the holes with wood glue. Insert the axle pin through the wheels and into the base holes.

Drill holes for the wheels.

7 Place a 1" mat board spacer on each side of the axle, between the wheel and the base, while gluing. After the glue dries, remove the spacers.

8 Attach a pull cord to the end or underside of the base at the front.

Sources: Sears® Craftsman® jig saw, JM Laminate, Michaels for wheels

Topper cat stool

Gare and Joan Hall have a great cat named Topper who sleeps on Joan's lap, races up and down stairs with Gare, and even rides on the front of their kayak. In this photo, Topper lazed on the kitchen chair. Because the viewpoint is looking down on the cat, it worked well to place the cat on a stool to view from the same perspective. This same pose would not have worked for the pull toy because of the viewpoint. If you have favorite photos you'd like to use, consider the viewpoint so the result looks logical.

Glue the cat onto the fabric-covered stool top.

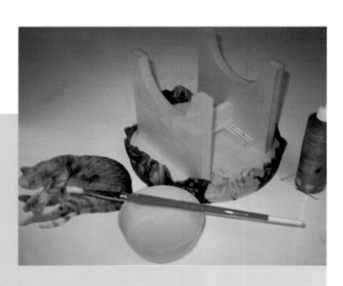

You need:
- Photo of pet or person from an overhead viewpoint
- Wooden stool 11" across round top
- Print fabric 18" X 42"

Supplies:
Acrylic paint, paintbrush, glue (Tacky Glue diluted), utility knife or razorblade, staple gun, 1/2" staples

1 Pick a photo shot from above, so your pet looks right on the stool. Photocopy it to size, about 8" x 9". Doctor the photo, if needed, with wax colored pencils (Eagle or Berol Prismacolor) to make eyes greener, sharpen detail, or repair his ear.

2 Laminate the cat and cut it out.

Unroll clear laminate paper onto the photocopy to protect the surface, or varnish the stool later.

3 Select a harmonizing fabric that does not overpower the photo. Cut out an 18" circle. Spread diluted white glue on the stool top, and smooth the fabric in place.

Spread white glue on the stool top.

4 Glue the stool edges, and firmly pull the fabric down over the rim to anchor it, smoothing out any wrinkles. Flip the stool over, and glue inward 1" around the rim. Push and pull the fabric toward the center to adhere the fabric and remove wrinkles. Use a razor blade or utility knife to trim the fabric 1" from the edge.

5 Flip the stool back to an upright position, and glue the cat onto the stool top.

6 Paint the edges of the stool base a harmonizing color. Varnish the entire stool and top, cat included, with water-base polyurethane. Let dry and add coats as needed.

7 To make the ruffle, cut three 8" x 24" strips of the same fabric used for the top. Sew the ends together and fold the strip lengthwise. Then fold and pin into 2 1/2" tucks to make a 34" circle. Staple the tucked ruffle to the underside of the stool top.

Once the glue has dried, fold tucks into the ruffle and staple around the top underside.

Sources: Michaels, JM Laminate, Tacky Glue, fabric designed by Richloom Fabrics®, Arrow® staple gun, Zar® clear wood finish polyurethane

Ian and Emily magnetic paper dolls

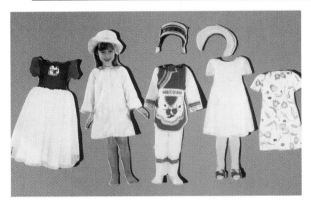

S tick these magnetic-backed paper dolls on your refrigerator door and change their clothes at will. The entire family can have a great time creating their own paper dolls. Here Emily and Ian Goodrich stood on a taped line on the stairs landing in their bathing suits and assumed the main pose. They alternated racing up stairs to change to a new outfit and dashing down again to assume the pose for the next shot. Any family member, including your cat or dog, could be the model (if you have a pet willing to dress up).

You can use the photos directly. These, however, were made with developed photos that were trimmed and grouped on paper, then photocopied larger. Their magnetic backing sticks to the refrigerator. You can also cut out tabs on the clothing and fold them down like old-time paper dolls.

You need:
- Camera, a point-and-shoot with flash is okay (Olympus 140 zoom used here)
- Paper
- Magnetic sheet with adhesive surface
- JM Laminate sheet
- Sharp, trimming scissors
- Color photocopier (or scanner, computer, and color printer)

Emily sticks to the refrigerator magnetically, where you can change her clothes daily.

1 Photograph the model in front of a light wall. Make all images the same pose and size, or the clothes won't fit. Tape a mark on the floor for the model. Mark another for the photographer, or use a tripod for the camera.

2 Dress the model in a body-hugging outfit, such as a bathing suit. (You'll have trouble getting films developed if the model wears less.) Decide on a pose, arms spread or on hips, and take two shots.

3 Change the model's outfit, assume the exact pose, and take two shots. Repeat for as many outfits as you wish.

4 On the photos, cut around the entire model figure. On the clothed photos, trim the background and body from the clothes. Mount these photos, ganged compactly, on paper. Color-photocopy it to 6" figures.

Cluster the trimmed photographs on paper.

Enlarge the cluster of photographs by photocopy.

5 Apply laminate on the front to stiffen and protect the dolls. Mount each on an adhesive-coated magnetic sheet, and cut them out with sharp scissors.

Mount the figures on a magnetic sheet.

Sources: Michaels or other crafts supply stores for Craft Magic® magnetic sheet (5" x 8") and JM Laminate, Kinko's for photocopies

Emily and Ian Goodrich posed for paper doll cutouts.

Using photos for crafts

69

71

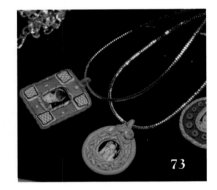

73

76

78

80

82

Goodrich badge

Second example by Leslie Masters Villani

Badges constitute awards for accomplishment or to celebrate special events. Those shown, both for 50th wedding anniversaries, also called for small size, since most people this age are trying to divest themselves of things. A friend made 50 sequined golden nametags for the Balmers' 50th anniversary party. The badge for Jack and Lois Goodrich is one of a kind and attests to his Scottish heritage. Both feature pictures of the couple's wedding day. You can make a playful, ornate, or dignified badge to commemorate a birthday, graduation, promotion, retirement, or simply a nice day if no event occurs. Official badges must follow prescribed form, but you can make yours any size, shape, or configuration you choose.

Celebrate any event, such as a 50th wedding anniversary, with a special "old time" badge to commemorate the occasion.

You need:

To make the green badge:

- Can lid 2 1/4" across
- 2 yards of soft-green grosgrain ribbon 7/8" wide
- 18" white and gold ribbon 1 1/2" wide
- 15" plaid ribbon 7/8" wide
- 10" metallic, wire-edged, dark green and dark red ribbon 3" wide
- Faux jewels on wire stems
- Safety pin clasp
- 7" gold cord

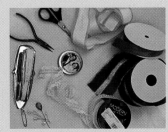

Gather your supplies to make a commemorative badge.

You need:

To make the gold badge:

- 4 1/2" metallic gold ribbon 1 3/4" wide
- Yellow Mylar plastic 1 1/4" x 6"
- Wooden heart 2" x 2"
- Pin back 1 3/8"
- Small cutout "50"
- 6" to 8" sequined braid 1/2" wide
- 12" thin florist's wire

Supplies:

Scissors, hot glue gun or white glue, staple gun, permanent marker, circle guide, jeweler's needle-nosed pliers, gold paint

1 Locate an old or new photo of the honoree that fits the occasion. Most old photos will be black and white. To add color, photocopy them on ivory colored paper and cover them with clear Mylar, or color the photocopy with Prismacolor wax pencils.

2 Use a circle guide or trace the heart to select the part of the photo to be cut out.

Use a circle guide to select the scene for the badge center.

3 For the ribbons, pleat the red and green ribbon in 3/8" folds, and thread a wire through the center to make a fan. Overlap ribbon ends and glue together. Thread the wire through one edge of the white and gold ribbon, pull to pleat and fan it. Flip half for a double fan.

Thread a wire through the center to fan the ribbon.

4 For the green rosette, fold nine 2" long loops of ribbon into a fanned circle and staple to hold.

To make the green badge

1 Assemble the parts from the bottom up before you glue or staple.

2 Fold 18" of green ribbon in half to make a top loop and tails for the backbone. Clip the ribbon to make angled tips.

3 Fold two 6" plaid ribbons into loops and staple them onto the green ribbon, 5" from the tips.

Staple the folded and pleated ribbons to the green base ribbon. Place the staples where added pieces will cover them.

4 Staple the white ribbon 1" down from the top.

5 Wire on the faux jewels.

6 Staple the rosette over the stapled joinings.

7 Glue the photo on the lid, and glue gold cord around it.

Staple the rosette ribbon in place, then add a ring of glue, and stick on the photo.

8 Glue the photo lid on the rosette.

9 Use a decorative brass safety pin in the top loop.

To make the gold badge

1 Paint the heart gold.

2 Cover the photo with transparent "gold" Mylar, cut both to shape and glue on.

3 Arrange the sequin braid to frame the photo, tuck in the thread ends of the braid, and glue in place.

4 Notch the gold and Mylar ribbons, and lay the Mylar on top.

5 Glue these to the heart back.

6 Letter the guests' names with permanent marker on gold Mylar ribbon.

7 Glue a pin back in place.

Sources: Jo-Ann, Hancock Fabrics, Michaels

Leslie Masters Villani made dozens of these name tags for a golden anniversary party.

Photo Art & Craft

Pose your friends and family to show their personality.

Fun figures

Polymer clay people

Clay is one of the first materials for child's play because it appeals to tactile and visual senses. It molds so easily into forms. Natural clay from the earth needs to be fired in a kiln at high temperatures to harden. Modeling clay with oil added becomes malleable but never hardens. Polymer clay is a plastic material that remains malleable and hardens when fired in a normal kitchen oven at 275 degrees. This clay comes in a variety of colors from subtle to wild. In this project, photo faces combine with poly clay figures to make funny little characters. Use them for place cards, gift decoration, toys, or collectibles.

Ross Hall played in the sand box in the original photo. Now his cutout face tops a kiddy car rider.

You need:

- Photos of faces
- A selection of polymer clay colors

Supplies and tools:

Clay, oven, modeling tools such as a paring knife, bamboo skewer, Tacky Glue, scissors

Dimensions:

3" to 4" tall

1 Choose small photos of people or pet faces. Use sewing scissors to carefully cut out the head.

2 To make the strongman, for example, roll a 1/2" ball of clay and flatten it to back the face. Put the face photo on it, and carve away extra clay.

Cutout photos top little clay figures of Dave Goodrich who likes to cook, Doug Stroud who likes to sail, and Garrett Hall who likes sports.

3 Mix colors, such as flesh and bronze, for the body clay. Knead to make the color you want. Roll balls for the tri-angular shape of the chest, the muscles, and the trunks.

Mix colors of clay for the flesh color you want, then roll balls and tubes to make the little figures.

4 Roll tubes for the legs, shoes, and arms. Bend the legs into feet and the arms to fists. To join pieces, press them together firmly enough to form a bond.

5 To bake or fire the figure, remove the photo and put the clay figure on a cookie sheet or foil. Preheat the oven or toaster oven to 275 degrees, and bake for 10-15 minutes, depending on the thickness of the clay. Watch to see that you don't overcook the figure or it will brown. Do not use a microwave oven.

Polymer clay models easily into little figures and bakes to hardness in the kitchen oven.

6 When cool, glue the photo on the head. You can embellish a figure with acrylic paints or varnish it with matte polyurethane.

Hattie Stroud uses the pasta machine to flatten the Sculpy III polymer clay into shapes for modeling.

Use polymer clay and photos of your best friends to create unique fashion accessories.

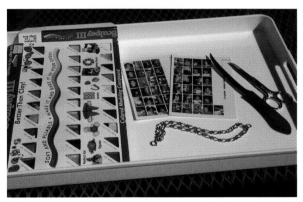

A white tray holds all you need to make polymer clay jewelry.

Jewelry

Portable art

Paper example by Leslie Masters Villani

Lockets with tiny photos inside have been popular since the advent of photography. Before that, hand-painted miniatures could show a king potential wives from distant royal families. Victorian-era gold lockets protected the photos within from wear and light fade. Contemporary jewelry can feature small photos too. Silver or gold metals rank highest with jewelers, since they are strong, malleable, and attractive. The home craftsperson has easier materials for making jewelry—polymer clay, wooden disks, or coated paper among them. They may not last as long as diamonds and gold, but they are fun for creating quick jewelry in passing styles.

You need:

For clay jewelry:

• Photo
• Polymer clay
• Clay tool (paring knife)
• Decorative cords or chain
• Aluminum foil 12" square
• X-Acto® knife
• Skewer
• Conventional oven or toaster oven

You need:

For paper jewelry:

• A small photo
• 2" and 1 1/2" card squares
• Decorative papers
• Two beads
• One plastic star
• White glue
• Pin back
• Red wire

For clay jewelry

1 Cut out a small photo of a grandchild, boyfriend, or special person. Cut the shape round, oval, or square to suit jewelry parts on hand (such as wooden disks) or mold the jewelry to fit the shape you cut.

2 Select the polymer clay colors that suit the photo.

3 Spread aluminum foil to work on. Roll and flatten a 1/2" ball of the base color, and place the photo on it. Trim the base to size and shape.

4 Press added decoration firmly onto the base.

5 For spiral trim, twist two or more thin rolls together. For checkerboard trim, use a pasta machine to roll 1/8" flat pieces. Stack the pieces, cut into strips, and flip every other strip to form a checkered cube. Stretch the cube smaller, and slice off thin squares.

6 To complete, make a clay loop for the cord, and press it firmly onto the base back.

7 Remove the photo before firing the piece. Bake for 10 to 15 minutes at 275 degrees. When cool, glue in the photo, and polyurethane the piece for durability.

Polymer clay can readily be modeled into tiny jewelry frames for little pictures. Add a loop for hanging.

Put the finished clay pieces on a foil-covered tray to bake.

Photo Art & Craft

For paper jewelry

1 Coat a 4" square paper with Elmer's glue to cover a 2" cardboard square. Fold the extra paper onto the back of the 2" square. On the reverse side, glue a 1 3/8" paper backing. Cover a smaller square with another color.

2 Assemble and glue the squares and added paper pieces as in Leslie Masters Villani's pin.

3 Thread the beads on the red wire. Wrap the square with the wire and beads. Tuck the wire end under the small square.

4 Slide the photo in place and glue.

5 Glue on a pin back with Tacky Glue.

Sources: Tacky Glue, Elmer's® Glue, Sculpy polymer clay, all from Michaels and Dick Blick

The proof print for a roll of pictures provided a good source for the tiny portrait of Sean Goodrich.

A small picture of Emily Goodrich tucked into Leslie Masters Villani's paper jewelry makes a cheerful, two-inch square pin.

A picture of Kyle Goodrich in a pendant-sized frame has an added piece on the back for a frame stand.

Using photos for crafts

Holiday faces

Ornaments

Ornaments can embellish a scene for any occasion. What a pleasure to look at the Christmas tree, a spring wreath, summer flowerpots, or the Thanksgiving centerpiece and see family faces smiling back. Ornamentation is often made from lightweight, colorful materials meant to be changed periodically and stored until their next seasonal appearance. The most common ornaments are fragile, glass holiday balls, but any shape will do to mount a family photo. Photos glued to flat disks are easiest to do; fitting a flat picture to the double curved surface of a ball requires more care.

Photo ornaments decorate this spruce tree.

You need:

- 3" glass ornament
- Photocopy of image
- Photographs 4" x 6"
- Stapler
- Glitter
- Sequins
- Gold cord
- Bead

Supplies and tools:

Elmer's glue, scissors, hand stapler

Sparkles add flair after the small photos have been glued on.

To make the glass balls

1 Photocopy photos to about 1" or less in size. Cut them out with a tiny outline border for best effect.

2 Test fit the image to the ball. Larger images will wrinkle, so make cuts into the image along hidden lines (as shown in the long hair) to shape the image to the round surface.

3 Spread Elmer's glue on the back of the photocopy, and smooth it onto the ball. If some wrinkles are unavoidable on larger photos, cover them with cutout holly leaves. Embellish the rest of the ball with glitter, sequins, or other trim.

4 Use a sponge to gently wash off any extra glue. When dry, varnish the image with polyurethane.

To make the origami box

1 Choose a 4" x 6" photo with the main imagery in a band across the center of the photo.

2 Where the top and bottom 3/4" of the photo fold inward, images will be distorted. Divide the photo in four, and trace the pattern on the back to inscribe the fold lines.

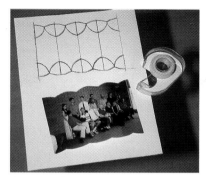

Draw the above pattern on the back of the photo and trim the scalloped edge.

3 Carefully fold along all of the lines, using the back of your fingernail to make a crisp edge. Clear tape the joining edges.

4 Push the folds inward to achieve the flower shape. Thread a bead stopper onto a tasseled cord, and string it through the box for an ornament. Or put a small gift inside the box for a treat.

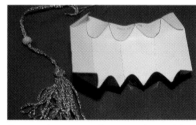

Crease the pattern lines as shown. The tassel with bead can string through the box for hanging.

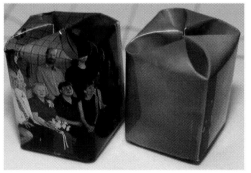

To make the chain

1 Use a paper cutter to cut each 4" x 6" photo crosswise into 4" x 1" strips or narrower.

2 With a hand stapler, loop a strip and staple the overlapping ends together. Loop the next strip through the first and staple.

3 Continue endlessly. This is a good use for poor photos.

Source: Michaels

Leslie's Lamp

Example by Leslie Masters Villani

Many people still take slides. Artists take them to submit their works to exhibition juries. Some artists use slides as a reference, projecting shots to see details from a scene or to achieve correct proportions in a painting. The publisher of this book needs slides for quality and detail when reproducing photo illustrations. Eventually this will be done with digital cameras, but technology, of the necessary quality, isn't yet widespread. Artist Leslie Masters Villani has lots of slides from travels, local scenes, and art entries. Most of the time her slides sit unseen in boxes. Ever inventive, she made a lampshade of slides, so she can see favored scenes whenever she passes by.

If you have boxes of scenic slides stored away, here's an inventive use for them.

You need:

- 154 slides
- 7 or 8 photos
- Drum-shape, white, lamp shade 14"x 16"
- Lamp 36" tall
- 60 feet of 12-gauge brass wire
- 200 white ceramic tiles 1" square
- White grout

Supplies:

Tacky Glue or acrylic glass medium, 3/8" dowel, wire cutters, needle-nosed pliers, leather punch or paper punch, snap clothes pins

"O" jump rings join the hole-punched slides.

1 Collect 154 slides of colorful scenes (or as needed) to cover the shade. Punch a hole in the center of each side of every slide mount. Use a paper punch on plastic slide mounts, or a leather punch for cardboard.

2 To make the "O" jump rings, wrap brass wire around a 3/8" dowel and clip each circle with wire cutters. Make 230 rings, or as needed (ready-made jump rings are available at craft or jewelry supply stores).

3 Lay out the slides 22 across by 7 slides high. Join all the slides together with the jump rings. To open a jump ring, twist side-ways. Insert the ring between two slides, and twist back to close.

4 Strip the old fabric or paper off the shade, or leave a sheer white fabric in place. Drape the assembled slides over the lamp frame, and clothespin them in place on the top wire. Insert "O" rings through the top row of slide mounts, or, if the shade fabric remains, use monofilament thread to sew the slides to the lamp frame. Join the bottom row of slides to the frame.

5 Shown is a ready-made lamp 36" high with a column base 4" diameter by 15". The base is covered with photos mounted on tiles. To achieve this effect, glue tiles on the base column, and fill the cracks with grout.

6 Cut seven or eight 4" x 6" photos into 1" squares, glue them on the tiles, and polyurethane varnish the base.

———

Sources: Home Depot for tools and supplies, Target® for a lamp

The base of a lamp was covered with tiles and grouted.

Leslie Masters Villani shows the drum-shaped lampshade made with her slides.

Grandmother clock

Time to see the grandkids, and there they are on the clock. Lacking twelve grandchildren, I used duplicate pictures of the grandchildren at different ages. Of course, the kids count their frequency of appearance on the clock, so you just have to tell each child privately that he or she is the most adorable one, which is true. School pictures used in several photos are a good size and clarity for the clock. If you want to save the original photos for your album, lay the photos on a page and color photocopy them. Here, the photos were cut to size to cover the numbers. But leave them exposed with a different arrangement if you wish. You can find an inexpensive clock in the drug store.

If you don't see enough of the grandchildren, put their faces on the clock and see them all the time.

Use a circle guide to cut out the faces, and colorful circles for added decoration.

You need:

- One clock 9 1/2" across with removable "crystal"
- 12 pictures of faces that fit within a 1 1/2" circle

Supplies:

Colored paper, white paper, circle guide, ruler, pencil, scissors, white glue

1 Select one large or 12 small photos of grandkids.

2 Pry the clear plastic "crystal" off the clock. Measure the size photo you need to cover the numbers, 1 1/2" as shown.

3 Use a circle guide to trace a 1 1/2" circle on each photo face. Use sharp scissors to cut out each photo circle. Touch up the backgrounds with markers or watercolor.

4 Arrange the photos by age of child, visual weight of photo, or some other design scheme, and glue them onto the clock face. Place the photos in a circle covering each number, or add colored paper circles, sequins, or other embellishments, and place them all randomly. Make sure all pieces are glued flat to avoid obstructing the hands' movement.

5 Replace the plastic cover, put in a battery, and hang the clock.

Sources: Clock from CVS/Pharmacy®, Michaels

Collect pictures of your grandchildren, mount them on paper, and photocopy them to save the originals.

Orchid table

This project is for dedicated crafters and jigsaw puzzle workers, but it's not difficult. The base for the photographic mosaic project is a black metal table found at a discount treasure store. The photographs show a collection of flower photos—orchids around the outside ring, garden flowers in the center. Photos cut into random-sized pieces can be fitted puzzle-style onto the tabletop, tray, box, or any object you'd like. Choose a limited color scheme in photos since the result can look quite chaotic. Putting in a contrasting circle of white paper chips organized this one. Any added paper pieces should be the same thickness as the photos. Varnish and you're done.

Tessera (glass tiles) are hard to cut for a mosaic table, but this mosaic made of photographs is easy.

You need:
- About twenty photographs 4" x 6"
- Table 24"
- Heavy paper

Supplies:
Spray paint (optional), Tacky Glue or decoupage glue, scissors, guide paper, compass, pencil, polyurethane varnish, brush

Gather a collection of related photographs. Loosely arrange them for effect.

1 Select a theme—flowers, faces, places, food, holidays, or an event. For a rainbow table, sort your stash of photos purely by color. Start with a purple ring 1/4" from the edge, add a blue ring within it. Continue with rings of green, yellow, orange, and red, to violet in the center.

2 Use the color of the table for "grout," or spray paint the table a color, such as white, taupe, or tan. Let the paint dry well.

3 On the heavy paper, draw a circle the size of the table. Measure 3 1/2" toward the center, and draw another circle. Make radiating lines across the circle, and cut out this shape as a template for the rim.

Make a template for cutting curved shapes.

4 Place the template over the rim photos to select photo parts. Trace the shapes and cut out each rim piece to fit 1/4" from the table edge. Cut sections across the ring or in any random shape (about 1" square).

Cut the photographs to the curved shape of the table, then cut across them toward the center for mosaic pieces.

5 Make smaller, ring-shaped templates for the other pieces as you move toward the center. Leave 1/8" to 1/4" between all mosaic pieces.

Arrange all the pieces before gluing them on.

6 If the design looks chaotic add a solid-color ring 1" wide. Clip across the paper ring at 1" intervals. Measure in accurately from the edge to fit pieces into a ring.

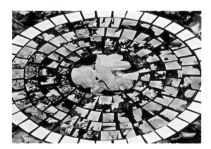
A ring of white paper squares helped organize this tabletop.

7 Lay out all pieces before gluing.

8 If needed, shift the pieces and trim them, so that rings are accurate and pieces are spaced evenly.

9 When all mosaic pieces are arranged, glue them in place one at a time. Brush on two coats of clear matte or satin-finish varnish.

Sources: Table from Tuesday Morning, Michaels

Chapter Five

Turning photo images into art

85

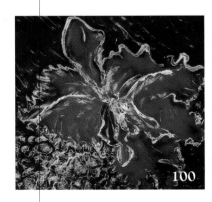

87

89

92

94

96

98

100

102

104

Flat drawings, paintings, and photographs are illusions of three-dimensional scenes. Here, added lines extend the market-scene photograph.

Market Day

Expanding the illusion

How amazing that the camera, like your eye, can turn a scene of real objects such as stones and trees, people and buildings into lines and colors on flat paper. The texture and smell of the moment is gone, but the imagery is saved in a way you can access at will. Artists delight in creating these illusions on paper, renderings that sometimes seem more real than the real thing. They play with these created illusion-images, sometimes overlaying one with another, sometimes combining two techniques. The aim in part is to cause you to recognize the illusion and to delight in the way scenes can be manipulated.

You can borrow from old masters such as Van Gogh. This half-finished piece uses his lively style in oil crayons to pick up the swirl of the iris plants in the photo.

You need:

- A selected photo
- Artist's paper, heavyweight
- Frame
- Mat board
- Foam core backing
- Clear plastic for frame

Supplies and tools:

Black ink, artist's brush, spray glue, picture hook and wire, staple gun, mat cutter, soft HB or 2H pencils

Dimensions:

11" x 17", paper 22" x 28"

1 Choose a photo scene that can be projected beyond its confines. Here a cluster of vegetables implies a market full of displays. Photocopy it to maximum size, 11" x 17", or as suits your design concept. For a larger piece, join two copies.

2 Select good quality, heavyweight art paper with a surface texture that will take pencil, ink, or crayon marks well. Some textures are smooth, others have "tooth" (a grainy quality that lends a different character to your lines).

3 Place the copy on the art paper, and plan where and how to expand the scene. Center placement gives stability. Off-center placement will be less static. Try sketches on newsprint first to see what achieves your goal.

4 Cover the photocopy back with spray glue. Align two corners, and roll the copy onto the paper, smoothing out air and wrinkles as you unroll. Some glues allow for repositioning; some stick forever on the first try.

5 Use black ink and brush, or HB pencil, to expand the scene. Sketch lightly with 2H pencil, draw over with ink, and when dry use a gum eraser to remove pencil lines. Step back as you work. Many artists work standing for free movement and a better view.

6 Select an appropriate frame. Visit a frame shop with a wide choice of mat color and frame stock, or buy a less expensive ready-made frame at a decorator store. Larger frames now more commonly use the lighter-weight, clear plastic instead of glass. It may scratch, but it won't break.

Sources: Home Goods or Pier One® for frames, Dick Blick or art store for paper and paint

In this experiment, oil crayons are applied directly to the photocopy to give an added layer to the already-layered water scene.

Photo Tip — *The camera as artist's tool*

You can use pictures to portray a message that you want the world to know. Photo artists use the camera as an artistic tool, manipulating the light, focus, character, expanse, and other aspects to create memorable photographic art works. It takes the same selective eye to frame the scene in a photograph as it does to design a painting. An artwork turns out better when you know what you aim to achieve.

A series of photos, taken at the Saturday morning market in Sarasota, provided imagery for more than one photo project—Market Day (project #33) and the Decoupage plates (project #12). Taking a series of scenes just for visual excitement may later be useful as ideas for any number of projects. Or go on a specific "shoot," aiming to express a particular idea as in the Edison poem (project #34). Treat your camera as an artist's tool, and enjoy the creative potential.

Edison poem

Message art

"A thing of beauty is a joy forever," one poet said. This picture poem carries a different message. Every time the power company comes through our yard to hack up the trees, we go out to supervise like angry crows at marauders. Their mission is to chop off everything to at least ten feet from the lines, no matter whether it's a slow-growing oak or a fast-growing silver maple. Outrage! And yet, here I sit at my computer using power to write. Outage! No power, no typing. Hence, this picture poem about the power line problem.

One sunny day, I followed the power company's trim path and photographed the butchered trees. Six of these photos were arranged horizontally with the perspective point—the direction of the road—toward the center to unify the group. The scene looks pictorially pretty at first, and then you see the exposed tree skeletons. Across the bottom are lines of a parody on Joyce Kilmer's poem "Trees." "Landscape" by Detroit Edison goes "I think that I shall never see/A poem as lovely as a tree/Unless of course it come to me/Through power lines to my TV."

You need:

- A series of photos
- Frame: Ready-to-assemble, black metal in two 12" pieces and two 40" sections
- Backing: 6 pieces 1/4" foam board 12" x 7 1/2"
- 6 strips of colored paper 1 1/2" x 8 1/2"
- White pencil
- 86" of picture wire

Tools:

Paper trimmer or cutter, white pencil, tiny Allen® wrench to assemble frame (or tool as specified), spray glue, gum eraser

1 Take a series of photos that tells your story. Compose each photo so the over-all design helps to carry your message. Plan ahead or let your pictures tell you what will be the most effective arrangement. Photocopy them to size, here 8 1/2" x 11", and arrange them in sequence.

2 Spray-glue the back of a photocopy, and mount it vertically on the foam board panel. Roll the copy downward, smoothing wrinkles as you go, then rub it firmly to adhere completely. Wrap the copy edges around the panel.

3 Hand letter or typeset your message across the center on each color strip. Include the title, your four poem lines, and your signature. Spray glue the back of each color strip, and mount them, over-lapping the photocopy at the base.

4 Using a pre-cut frame kit, assemble two sides and the bottom. Fit the right side panel in first, and then overlap successive panels to fill the frame. Fit the frame top in place, and insert backing or braces.

5 Adjust the wire carriers, and add a doubled wire.

Sources: Frame kits from Dick Blick, art stores, Michaels

The Edison poem, a protest artwork entitled "Landscape by Detroit Edison," looks pretty enough at first sight, until you see the mutilated trees in the tree trimmers wake.

The Mask Quilt contains twenty-eight masks that were photographed and transferred onto fabric blocks.

The size of smaller masks was increased with additional sashing strips. Mask squares in horizontal rows organized the quilt design.

Mask Quilt

Use your collection

The photocopy transfer technique is an easy way to apply imagery to fabric. Quilters appreciate being able to borrow photographic imagery to create their own fabric designs. This quilt shows a collection of masks gathered on foreign travels. The fabrics surrounding the masks also came from near and far, from old and new, hinting at the mask's cultural background. A mask beguiles all by itself, but, combined with fabrics, ceremonies, and folklore, it becomes a more dramatic object. Showing that was the aim of this quilt.

You need:
- 25 + photos
- 25 off-white cotton fabric blocks 9" x 12" (cotton polyester fabrics are also acceptable)
- A fabric stash for sashing
- Fiberfill quilt bat 50" x 70" (single bed size)
- Backing fabric 50" x 70"
- Photo transfer paper

Supplies and tools:
Presser or iron, sewing machine, sharp scissors, ruler, matching threads, hand quilting needles, and threads

Dimensions:
49" x 68" quilt

1 Take photos from your collection, or shoot a planned series on a related subject. This quilt's 25 blocks feature 28 masks. You can assemble photos first and design the quilt from there, as with this quilt, or plan the quilt and take the photos for specific places.

2 Photocopy the images on special photo-transfer paper. This must be fed through a color copier, or done at an office supply store. You can reduce or enlarge photographs during this step. Photo transfer paper costs about $3.00 per sheet, so test the color and size of photographs first by copying them on regular copy paper.

3 A list of recommended photocopy machines is included in the transfer paper package. Be sure to follow the directions on the package when you use the photo-transfer paper. Remove photos from frames before copying, and place photographs face down in the color copy machine. For maximum use of the transfer paper, group the photos on 8" x 11" paper.

4 Use white or light-colored, tightly woven fabric. A cotton-poly combination worked best for me, but test various fabrics for best results. Do not pre-wash fabric; it lays smoother right off the bolt, and the photo-transfer process will stabilize the fabric. Cut the fabric into blocks.

5 Cut each image from the transfer paper. For hand or machine appliqué, you need not trim exactly to shape. Position the image face down on the fabric quilt block. Use a press set at 375 to 400 degrees or an iron set at its hottest (no steam). Press, don't iron, the photo-transfer image for 25 to 30 seconds, using maximum pressure. Check the fabric back to see if it adhered well (the design shows through more).

The Mexican mask on the left was photographed, cut out, and transferred to white fabric.

6 Peel the photo-transfer paper from the fabric immediately, while the paper is still hot. If you have trouble, reheat it for a few seconds before peeling again. If needed, cover with backing paper and iron lightly to smooth out any distortions. Photo transfers are now permanent; you can sew or iron directly on the images. You can wash completed photo-transfers.

7 Lay out your blocks, and assemble a stash of possible fabrics for sashing. Here, Indonesian batiks, African prints, and Oriental designs frame the masks from those countries. Some fabrics of mixed and unknown origin were used because the color and design were right. Design the quilt in strips to organize. Start at the top strip and design downward. Repetition of fabrics (note the "tiger stripe") gives cohesion to a chaotic design. Be cautious of primary colors, since they overwhelm the more subtle transferred photos.

Fabrics related to the masks' origins are used for sashing as well as appliquéd onto the quilt.

8 Hand quilting the masks gives a puffy, three-dimensional effect, but transfer-coated fabric is more difficult to stitch than soft cotton. Use sharp quilting needles and leather thimbles, one on each hand, to protect your fingers. Use quilting thread to match the background or the mask border. This quilt includes both hand and machine quilting.

This ancient Japanese mask "The god who eats the moon" is hand quilted to give a raised trapunto effect.

Sources: Photo-transfer paper from Clotilde®; Martingale & Co.®, P.O. Box 118, Bothell, Wash. 98041, (800) 426-3126; Nancy's Notions quilt catalogs; art stores; Hancock fabrics. For more detail on making quilts see: Maggi McCormick Gordon, *Pictorial Quilting* (Watson-Guptill Publications, 2000). Or try these titles published by Krause Publications: *All Quilt Blocks Are Not Square* by Debra Wagner; *Fast Patch: A Treasury of Strip Quilt Projects* by Anita Hallock; *Fine Hand Quilting* by Diana Leone and Cindy Walter.

Masks shown here are from Africa and Bali (above), Japan and Indonesia (left), and Italy and Africa (below).

Collage quilt

Photo Collage

Quilt by Kathleen Field

Kathleen Field experiments with overlaying images on top of each other to achieve her effects. She asserts that these are art quilts, meant to hang on the wall.

Using collage, Kathleen Field applies contemporary graphic techniques to the age-old craft of quilt making. These art quilts differ from the average pieced quilt in purpose. She says, you don't take art quilts off the bed and toss them in the washer; they are meant to be hung as serious art works. She transforms photocopied images and related text by enlarging, reducing, and manipulating them to create her collages. Just as paintings do, her quilts all have strong messages that are conveyed through visual imagery.

Field creates collages from bits of photographic imagery, other collected images, torn papers, and text. Not limited to photographic imagery, she borrows any image from throughout the ages to illustrate her concept. Early on, she tried making fabric collages and enlarging them 400% to make large quilts. This resulted in color and image distortion, so she works now with paper collages first. Then she enlarges the collages using a photocopier and applies them to fabric. She exhibits these works widely at museums, galleries, and art fairs.

You need:
- A collection of photos
- Borrowed imagery
- Text

Supplies and tools:

Photo transfer paper, sketch paper, scissors, ruler, glue, photocopier; light-to-white, firmly-woven fabric

Dimensions:

Choose your own size

This process is called photo heat transfer to differentiate it from photo emulsion printing, blue printing, screen-printing, or other fabric transfer techniques. Adhering imagery to fabric changes the "hand" or feel of the fabric, so a tightly-woven, smooth fabric is used. This technique also stabilizes the fabric, often a good trade-off.

Field makes collages of photographs and other visuals for her small quilts.

1 Plan your visual story. Use whatever flat, visual imagery carries out your ideas. Assemble photographic images, graphic images (art book pages, magazine images, photos of your paintings), textured papers, or text.

2 Arrange and rearrange the pieces of your collage until you achieve the result you want. Some hints: Cut images into sections and intersperse them into the collage. To create levels in the scene, overlay images so no white background remains. Repeat images in various sizes for a sense of rhythm. Use torn edges to get away from rigidity. Superimpose decorative design elements as needed to balance the scene and guide the viewer's eye. Use any design technique that comes to mind to create your collage.

3 Photocopy the resulting collage on transfer paper (in reverse if text is included). Copy it in sections if it exceeds the transfer paper size.

4 Position the transferred images onto the background fabric. Use tape or pins to stabilize while ironing. Press, don't iron, to adhere (see Mask Quilt, project #35). Peel the backing off while it's still hot.

5 To assemble the quilt, either frame the printed blocks with added sashing pieces, or hem the collage edges and appliqué the piece into the quilt face.

Sources: Transfer paper from Clotilde, Nancy's Notions quilt catalogues, or office supply stores

Field says—now that she has mastered the technique of enlarging paper collages and transferring them to fabric—in her new project, she can reduce the collages and make "Little Quilts."

Dream house

Sculpture

For years I've dreamed of houses. Most often, they are small houses that open up inside to enormous spaces that I can furnish. It's not too hard to decipher that one with dream interpretation—endless possibilities. Since my house dreams are largely hopeful, I look forward to their unpredictable appearance.

Tired of waiting for the next dream, I decided to make my own dream house, not of bricks and mortar, but boards and metal. The house is sheathed in copper roofing, weathered to a beautiful patterned patina. The windows enclose photographs of people at a gallery opening where my artwork won an award. The small size of the windows and people within gives the house scale. It is inscribed with sayings about houses and homes; on the front is written, "The shape of my house is a dream—endlessly repeated, endlessly variable—a metaphor for possibilities," on

Copper-clad "Dream House" shows photos of people in the windows to give implied scale to the sculpture.

one side it says, "Home is where the art is," and on the other side "Home is not where you live but where they understand you."

You need:

- House: 1/2" particle board 36" x 48"
- Roof: 24" of 1/4" x 3 1/2" lath or rough siding
- Cladding: Copper roofing sheet 30" x 48"
- 2 photos 3"x 3"
- Doll house cupboard 4" x 6 1/2" x 1 1/2"

Supplies and tools:

Acrylic paint, polyurethane varnish, 1 1/2" finishing nails, 1" brads (small head), copper nails, wood glue, Tacky Glue, power saw, tin snips, hammer, right angle, ruler, pencil, rubber mallet

Dimensions:

House 10" wide x 5" deep x 45" tall

1 Select photos that are related to the sculpture concept to fit into the windows of the dollhouse architecture—in this case, a cupboard.

2 For the house sheathing, use a weathered piece of copper roofing, or paint the surface. If you choose to paint the sheathing, mix acrylic paint into washes of blue-green, purple, and brown to get the natural patina colors formed when various chemicals oxidize with the copper. Pour a color on, shift the metal to make natural patterns, and let dry. Repeat for each color.

3 To build the house framework, cut two strips 10" x 45" of 1/2" particleboard for the front and back. Measure down 3" on each side. Draw and cut lines to the center to make the top roof peak. For the sides, cut two strips 4" x 42". For the base, cut a 4" x 9" board. For the roof, cut four sheets of rough siding 3 1/2" x 6". To assemble, nail or screw the front to the sides, the base to the front and sides, and join the back.

4 Align the copper vertically to the right side at the rear corner, and use a row of copper nails to join. Roll the house to fold the copper around the corner to the front. Pound the copper with a rubber mallet to mold the corner fold. Roll again to crease, and pound to fit. Roll to crease to the

back, pound to fit copper ends snugly at the corner, and join with copper nails on the back.

7 Using tin snips, cut the roof copper gable to fit. Glue the roof boards on the gable and nail with brads.

8 Align the doll cupboard on the front, and Tacky Glue in place.

9 Trim the photos, back them with mat board to stiffen, and fit them into the windows.

10 Use acrylic paint to inscribe sayings on the house. Spray with polyurethane to protect the patina surface.

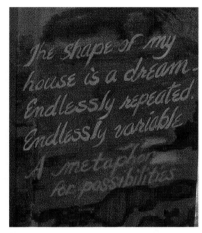

Sayings about houses embellish the building sides.

Sources: The Home Depot or lumber yard for wood; Liquitex® acrylic artist colors from Dick Blick, Michaels, or art stores

Open the tiny windows to see a group of women artists inside.

NYC building

Point of view

What is perspective? Simply, it means point of view. Visual perspective in a picture shows angle and distance as it appears to the eye (or the camera). Distant objects appear smaller, close ones larger. Mental perspective means to view from a particular standpoint— "In my perspective …." My aim in this wall hanging was to combine both meanings. Starting at the bottom of the building, I took several shots, aiming each farther upward from my street-level standing point to show the distortions of perspective that our brains are able to filter out.

Most photos are taken at eye level, aiming forward. Knowing this allows the viewer to orient to the scene. For a different perspective, give a camera to a child who aims up at adults or ignores the concept of a level horizon. Take a photo from an airplane for a bird's eye view.

Multiple photos of this New York building show changing perspective as the camera moves up and the viewpoint changes.

Snap overlapping shots while turning around 360 degrees for a surround perspective. To experience changing perspective the next time you see a movie, note where the camera is situated.

In this wall hanging, a series of photographic views are sewn to canvas and assembled into a long strip.

You need:

- 7 photographs 8" x 10"
- Cotton canvas 60" x 16"
- Backing fabric (brown print) 60" x 16"
- Bonded fiberfill batting 60" x 16"
- 21 purple beads
- 21 dark blue beads
- 220 light blue beads
- 15" board (lath 1 1/2" x 1/3")
- White and black thread

Supplies and tools:

Ruler, scissors, sewing machine, beading needle, darkroom enlarger, pencil

Dimensions:

5" x 52" x 1/2"

1 Plan a series of shots that overlap vertically. The subject can be a building, tree, person, or whatever object causes you to marvel at the height. Enlarge the photos to 8" x 10". Trim the photos to show only the central object. Arrange them so they almost join in a vertical strip. The shots do not need to mesh perfectly where they join. Like a movie, these represent a series of views.

2 Cut the face canvas and backing fabric to size.

3 On the face canvas, draw a box to fit your photos (here 11" x 48" with borders 2 1/2" inches from each edge, 3" from the bottom, and 9" from the top). The top folds over for the rod pocket.

4 Free-motion machine stitch your story around the edges. To do this, guide the fabric with no feed dog action and little pressure from the presser foot. Set the machine to darn, if there's no pressure

control. The needle is your pencil point as you move fabric under it to form the letters. Sew at a fast speed with slow movement to form tiny stitches and avoid breaking the needle.

5 Sew the canvas to the backing face to face, adding fiberfill 2" wide around the edges, and turn right side out. Topstitch a border 2" on each side and 3" at the ends.

6 Lay the canvas flat to tape the photos in the center. Use the sewing machine to sew around each photo edge to anchor them. Be sure to use a long stitch to avoid over-perforating the photos.

7 Hand sew the beads in the sky.

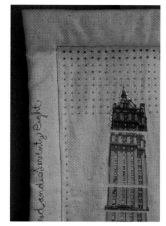

The top of the wall hanging is further embellished with sky-blue beads hand-sewn in orderly rows at the top.

Sources: Hancock fabrics, Kodak

Rock banner

Close-up for texture

As so often happens in designing an artwork, one choice or decision helps make, or even insists upon, the next. Once focused on the rock detail, selecting handmade textured papers to go with the enlarged photocopies was a given. The photos and fragile papers are backed with fabric, suggesting they be sewn together, quilt fashion. Leaving exposed seams on the wall hanging face protected the paper surfaces from sharp folds and provided shadows for delineation.

The varied rock surfaces, combined with their mass, inspired this wall hanging to show their force.

You need:
- 8 photocopied images
- One mauve handmade paper 38" x 20"
- One gray handmade paper 10" x 25"
- Canvas for backing 36" x 48"
- Threads

Supplies and tools
Serger or sewing machine, needle, thread, scissors, paper cutter, dowel rod, cord

Dimensions
Overall 31" x 39"

Move in closer on a scene like this for rock details and textures.

1 Take a series of close-up nature prints, so only the detail of the object shows. Rock surfaces become patterns resembling aerial maps or woven tweed fabrics.

Handmade papers show similar textures to the rock surfaces, yet display their contrasting characteristics.

2 Enlarge the photos by color photocopy to 8 1/2" x 11". Make more than eight prints to give yourself choices.

3 Arrange the prints for best effect. To frame the prints with paper sashing, cut strips of handmade paper 1 1/2" to 2" wide.

4 Cut a doubled paper strip for the rod pocket at the top, 6" wide and 31" long, side strips 3 1/2" x 37", and a bottom strip 4" x 25" as shown. Cut matching canvas backing strips for each of these pieces and the photocopies.

5 Set your serger to a long, overcast stitch to avoid over-perforating the paper. On a sewing machine, use an overcast stitch that does not curl the edges. Join the canvas-backed frame strips to the canvas-backed print sides first.

The photocopies of the rocks and paper sashings are all backed by canvas to strengthen the serged seams.

6 Join the canvas-backed center strip to both prints. Flatten the seam toward the thinner paper. Join the assembled top row to the second row, the second to the third, and the third to the bottom strip.

7 Join the canvas-backed side strips to the joined center strips.

8 Sew the ends of the canvas-backed top strip, fold double to make a rod pocket, and join to the hanging. Insert a dowel rod in the rod pocket at the top, tie on a cord, and hang.

Sources: Dick Blick for papers, Hancock or Jo-Ann for fabrics

Photo Tip

BIG! Some of the enormous rocks used as retaining walls between our condo units measure four feet across and must weigh tons! The scale of close-up photos pictured their immensity best. Bigness or scale is a tool artists use for effect. Think of Andy Warhol's Campbell Soup cans. He painted an ordinary four-inch product to three feet or more, using enormous scale to change the subject from commonplace to remarkable. Increasing size and zeroing in on detail alters the focus.

See that rock or bush in your front yard? Move in close with your camera to discover design and texture. The palm bush, shown in project #4, shows this clearly. Move in close to eliminate the background and see the patterns. The closer you get, the more abstract in design the image grows, becoming lines and patterns, shadow and light, textures and colors. For very close-up shots, you will need a close-up or macro lens for your SLR camera. Most cameras cannot focus closer than 30".

Close-ups

Move in close to the rock and suddenly its surface becomes a complicated pattern of colors and textures.

Polaroid prints

Image transfers

Works by Jane Letchworth, Megan Butler, Bob Vigiletti, and Ken Vigiletti

Jane Letchworth manipulated the Polaroid, dye-transferred surface by hand.

Click, whirr, wait a minute and a half, and you have an instant photograph taken by Polaroid camera, a device invented by Dr. Edwin Land in the 1960s. Each exposure in the film packet contains a light sensitive negative containing dyes, a positive emulsion for the image, and a pod of reagent to develop one picture sandwiched between lightproof papers. The whirring noise occurs when the rollers squish the developer packet. Artists use photo-transfer techniques, a crossover art form in which a technical method of reproducing scenes is combined with handcraft techniques, for artistic effect.

The two main techniques of Polaroid transfer require Polaroid Polacolor ER print film. In the first technique, called image transfer, the Polaroid photo is pulled apart during developing, and the negative is pressed on paper to transfer the dyes for a soft water-color effect. The second technique transfers the developed Polaroid emulsion from the negative and paper backing to another surface. The result is more detailed and colorful than the image transfers using dyes.

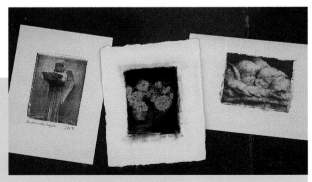

Instant Polaroid photos contain their own developing dyes that can be transferred to watercolor paper, as shown in these prints by Jane Letchworth.

You need:
- Polaroid Polacolor ER film extended range
- A camera with a Polaroid film pack holder
- An enlarger or a slide printer (Vivitar slide printer and/or Dylab Jr. slide printer)
- Watercolor paper, handmade paper, or other surface

Technique One:

1 Shoot or print a Polaroid photo. You can compose the scene in the camera viewfinder, with the enlarger, or with the slide printer.

2 Pull apart the negative and emulsion after 15 seconds, before the film develops fully.

3 Place the negative with the dyes face down on hot, soaked watercolor paper, and press lightly with a brayer (roller). The dyes continue to develop and transfer to the paper. Squeegee by hand to remove excess water. Peel off and discard the negative, which can make only one print.

4 Embellish the watercolor print by scraping away or adding color and lines as in any painting.

Technique Two:

1 Take or print a Polaroid photo. Compose the scene in the camera viewfinder, by the enlarger, or with the slide printer.

2 Soak the fully developed print in hot water. Rinse with cold water to separate it from the backing. Float the emulsion off the backing onto another surface. Bob Vigiletti transferred this fragile emulsion film onto the double-curved surface of an egg for exquisite results.

Other Techniques:

Polaroid film size is so small that some artists transfer and manipulate the emulsion as in the first two techniques, add other effects, then photograph the result. They expose and print an enlarged image on photographic paper or other light-sensitized surface. Photo paper comes in a variety of surface finishes from glossy to matte, and from smooth to linen textured.

Sources: Polaroid Transfers by Kathleen Thormond (Amphoto, 1997). Vivitar or Dylab, Polaroid (provides instruction sheets)

Megan Butler experiments with the Polaroid technique by transferring a colorful church window to paper she made.

Photo by Robert Vigiletti

Robert Vigiletti used a different Polaroid transfer technique to apply the film emulsion itself to an egg.

Photo by Robert Vigiletti

Robert's son Ken Vigiletti used a third technique to glorify his baby. He manipulated the emulsion then photographed it, enlarging the result.

Picture poems

Photosensitive prints

By Judy Clark Lindberg

To banish doubt that photography qualifies as art, look at Judy Clark Lindberg's framed pieces. She uses photographic imagery combined with other artistic elements such as handmade watercolor paper, handmade paper mats, metallic framing, and other embellishments. Further, she includes a few lines of printed text stating her philosophy. There's more. Sewing machine stitchery affixes the textured inner mat containing the text to the background. Macramé knotting and beaded cord for a swag hang from a short wooden rod with a small dangling charm. Too much? No. From here she hand colors the black and white photographic imagery.

Once Lindberg has developed her imagery to this point, she can run an edition, meaning

Photo courtesy of Judy Clark Lindberg

Judy Clark Lindberg applies a photo-sensitive emulsion to watercolor paper, exposes and develops the image, then hand colors it.

a limited number of prints. A photo enlarger was used to expose and print the image on handmade paper. Each print is hand colored, providing opportunity for experimentation.

You need:

- Liquid Light Emulsion
- Darkroom facilities (no matter how modest), including a photo enlarger
- Handmade paper (or other surface)
- Dyes

To make the frame:

- Metal frame 16" x 20"
- Hand-made paper 6" x 7 1/2"
- Foam core 5 1/2" x 7"
- White textured paper 7" x 11"
- Colored and textured background 11" x 14"
- Backing 16" x 20"
- Textured mat 16" x 20"
- Foam board 16" x 20"

To create photo images on unusual surfaces such as textured papers, wood, or glass, you must work in a darkroom. A liquid emulsion is applied to the desired surface to make it photosensitive. Each of these surfaces presents different problems in trying to achieve the necessary smooth, even coating of emulsion. For example, glass resists it, and flexible fabric needs to be stretched taut. Even so, the results of printing a photo on barn wood or clear glass seem quite magical.

1 Begin with a black and white photo. You can add color later with dyes. Plan to work in a darkroom to avoid ambient light.

2 Select the printing surface such as handmade paper 6" x 7 1/2". Coat several sheets, including one for test strips, to determine correct exposure. Dip the paper in a pan of the mixed emulsion solution, and lay it on a flat surface tipped at an angle to drain. The emulsion can be brush-painted on wood, glass, or other material, but it must be smooth and evenly coated. Lay the printing surface flat and let it dry completely in the dark.

3 Position the photosensitive surface under the enlarger, and focus through a red-orange filter to project the size you

want. The surface must be flat or the print will be distorted.

4 Use a test strip with different time lengths to achieve the right exposure. Properly expose, develop the print, stabilize it in hypo solution, and then wash it in water. Now you can turn on the light to let it dry flat.

5 To add color, brush-paint or cotton swab with photo dyes. You can build up more intense color with successive layers, as well as mix colors or blend one color into another.

Sources: Dick Blick, Liquid Light Emulsion® (Rockland Colloid Corp. available at larger photo shops or in photo magazine ads), dyes from Kodak, Spotpen Inc.

Presentation lifts this artist's work out of the ordinary. Lindberg adds a line of philosophy and frames the work with multiple layers of matting.

Tulips

Screen print

Sometimes an artist starts with a technique and searches for photographic imagery to fit. These tulips growing in our front garden provided imagery for a photographic screen print. Screen-printing is a refined stencil technique in which the ink goes through the fine mesh screen areas not blocked off by the stencil. The stencil here is a coating of film adhered to fabric that has been stretched taut in a frame. This type of stencil can achieve much more detail than is possible with a stiff, cutout stencil. The ink is also applied differently. Pigmented ink, the texture of heavy cream, is poured into the screen frame and pulled across the design by a wide squeegee. This process is used to make everything from art prints to tee shirts.

The "Tulips" serigraph shows how photographs can be reduced to flat colors.

Commercially, it can be used to print on rounded surfaces such as glass tumblers, metal instruments, or even plastic signs.

The tulip imagery for screen-printing was reduced to flat tones for one color, or one run of the squeegee. Normally, a three-color print requires three different stencils and careful registration to align the colors. The tulip print was produced by squeegee-ing two colors at once, allowing them to blend in the center to make three colors—orange flowers, brownish stems, and green leaves.

You need:
- Black and white photograph and negative
- Darkroom enlarger
- Kodalith photo paper
- Framed printing screen, larger than the print
- Photo-sensitive screen printing film
- Oil-based screen printing ink in orange and green
- Squeegee as wide as the print
- Clean up supplies (mineral spirits and rags)
- Block-out paint to mend stencil
- Art paper
- Frame
- Backing

Dimensions:
Paper 24" x 30", image 15" x 22"

1 Photograph a scene that can be reduced to a black and white image. The first photo shows the tulips, the yard, and the neighbor's house. In the second, a white sheet blocks out the background. In the third, the camera moves closer to cut out the sheet holder and surroundings, picking up more detail on the flowers.

A first black and white shot of the tulips shows how they will look in limited color, but the photo has a complicated background.

2 Build or purchase a screen larger than the image with a 6" wide space at each end for the ink. Use 2" x 2" smooth lumber for the frame. To make the screen, stretch and staple a fine mesh fabric (organdy, silk, or polyester) across the bottom of the screen.

3 In the darkroom, paint the light sensitive emulsion on the screen and let it dry. Keep it in the dark.

4 In the darkroom, expose the photo negative onto Kodalith paper to eliminate gray tones. The result will be a full-size, high-contrast black and white picture to expose on a light-sensitive coated screen. In a second, shorter technique, expose the photo negative directly onto a screen-printing film with paper backing. Read the Kodalith package for complete details.

5 While it is still wet, apply the developed photosensitive film to the screen. Wash out the exposed area with hot water and a soft brush. Pull off the backing and let the screen dry.

6 To print a "run" of several prints, use hinges on the frame for accurate placement, and tape guides for paper placement on a flat, slightly padded surface.

7 Align the paper under the screen. Pour the oil-based, screen-printing ink into the frame at one side (orange at the top and green below are used here), apportioned evenly across, so all areas of the print will register clearly.

Turning photo images into art

8 Pull the squeegee, with the ink in front of it, across the screen once. The first print will show a demarcation where the colors meet. Subsequent prints will mix the two colors increasingly. Let the prints dry.

9 To clean the screen, pour and scrape out unused ink. Pour in mineral spirits, and rub with a rag in each hand to clean the front and back of the screen.

10 On the lower edge of the print, write the title on the left side, the print number in the center, and sign your name on the right. This print is numbered as S1, meaning the first state of printing. Using a different set of colors to print would be state two. The other numbers 1/10 mean the first of ten prints. Such a small run could also be titled "artist proofs" (AP) since they were experimental, each print varying some.

―――――

Sources: Kodak for film, Dick Blick for screen supplies; Ulano® inks, photosensitive films and tools, Strate-Edge squeegees, Drum-Tite printing frames and hinge clamps

Moving in closer, the camera picks up the row pattern of flower heads, stems, and leaves.

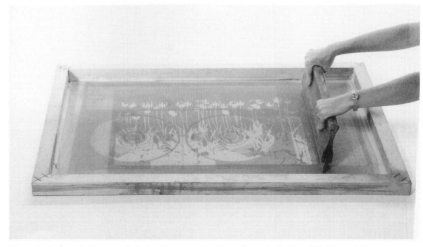

The photo has been made into a re-used screen for printing multiple copies.

Photo Art & Craft

Screen-printed art, called a serigraph, brings color to any room.

Turning photo images into art

107

Chapter Six

Using copier and computer

109

111

113

115

117

119

12

123

Photo Art & Craft

Computer art

Photos by Robert Vigiletti

The computer has a vast array of techniques for altering imagery. One technique called solarization, involves flashing the image with light in the photo developing process. The black and white merry-go-round prints by Bob Vigiletti show how the computer readily accomplishes this same eerie effect. Vigiletti experimented with three variations on this theme. The results are computer printed on watercolor paper, 11" x 14".

"Carrousel Horses" by Robert Vigiletti

The darkroom technique of solarization becomes quick and manageable by computer. Vigiletti printed out three different versions of "Carrousel Horses."

Photo Tip

Photo artists

"All the remarkable and unusual techniques we used to do in the darkroom," says Bob Vigiletti, founder of the Photography Department of Center for Creative Studies in Detroit, "can now be done on the computer. Where photographers spent hours in the darkroom printing, enlarging, and developing photos, they now spend time at the computer. Of course, many photographers still prefer their darkroom for some photo characteristics the computer does not have, particularly in producing art quality photographs. A background in hands-on darkroom work gives a better understanding of working on the computer."

A camera is still necessary to record the photo image that serves as a basis for enhancement by darkroom or computer. Following are a variety of ways to use the computer from the most minimal, setting type for paste-ups, to complete art works by computer.

Sedan Number 23
by Don Unwin:

Don Unwin does computer enhancement on his car photos, using computer graphic software to alter colors and increase contrast. What might have been an ordinary car photo, he says, turns out to be quite exciting in dazzling colors. He first scans the original photo into a computer software program for manipulating and then begins to experiment. Don Unwin created this artwork from what he calls a rather ordinary photograph. The exotic colored areas with granular looking edges, similar to the photographic solarizing technique, accomplish a sophisticated and intriguing effect.

Don gave the photo "pizzazz" by scanning the original into a digital format file with his Polaroid SprintScan™. Using Adobe® Photoshop 5.5®, he clicked on Image on the menu, then selected Curves. By moving a line up or down, he could change colors at will. When he was satisfied, he saved the image shown (top), a prizewinner.

Don Unwin scanned an ordinary photo into his computer, enhanced it with "pizzazz," and won an award on the framed result.

Unwin, a car buff, shot this photo of a classic car, but he considered the result ordinary.

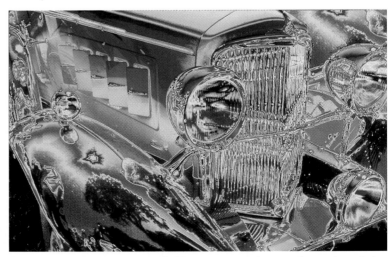

Showing what the computer can do, Unwin moves in closer on the previous photo and flips the photo to manipulate the colors and textures with dazzling effect.

Photo Art & Craft

Hall family cards over four years show similar design but varying text formats, including doggerel poems, headlines, and captions.

The computer-literate Hall children do their cards by scanning photos into computer software programs, Claudia Hall Stroud's is shown above.

Anyone can easily make photographic holiday cards by the paste-up technique. Assemble the photos on a background (left), add some text, and have them photocopied.

Holiday cards

Paste-ups and layouts

Examples by author and family

Friends say they look forward to our Christmas cards, since they carry so much news. Our guidelines for producing family cards are: 1. Make sure everyone in the immediate family gets in at least one photo. 2. Each family gets one sentence of news—the pictures tell the rest. 3. The pictures chosen are action shots rather than posed studio pictures.

Computers can partly or entirely produce Christmas cards, birthday cards, or other messages. The cards in this project take the least computer skill. Computer generated text is combined with photographs, assembled by the layout paste-up technique, and printed by color photocopier. This technique does allow for easy, free-form arrangements and casual hand lettering, but it can also achieve neat typeset results, as shown, using rulers and T-squares.

You need:
- Collection of photos
- Text
- Several sheets of white paper

Supplies:
Clear tape, glue stick, scissors or paper cutter, ruler, small T-square or triangle

1 Sort through the past year's photos and choose shots that have a similar color range and size. Select lively scenes that tell the story, not stiff "I'm posing now" photos. Use standard photos direct from the developers, or have special sizes made if it's worth the effort for your concept.

2 For the layout, tape a 9" x 12" paper (1/2" frame included) to a flat surface with a straight edge on the side for the T-square.

3 To develop a design concept for the page, try various arrangements with the photos . Squint your eyes to reduce the page to shapes and colors, minus details, to evaluate the over-all design. Leave space for the text.

4 Write the text first and fit the photos around it, or select and arrange the photos to fit the text to them. Create the words in some form—as a poem, headlines, quotes, captions, or whatever works for your idea. Choose a computer font and size, or hand letter your text. Since people often put newsletters aside to read later, if at all, edit your copy down to as few words as possible. You can always add a page of news for close friends.

5 Use the T-square or triangle to align the photographs. The photos can overlap one another or go off the paper edge to focus on the section you want. Or trim them to size. Clear-tape the photos in place where the tape won't show.

6 Overlay the text, and glue-stick or tape it down. Add paper strips to frame the scene and cover unwanted photo areas.

7 Photocopy the paste-up at an office shop, such as Kinko's, Office Depot, or Office Max. The photocopier leaves a white border, so you may need to reduce the paste-up to fit. Print the number of cards you want at about $1.00 each.

8 Sign your name on the text before copying, or leave space and hand sign it for a personal touch. Fold the card in three for a standard business size envelope, or buy larger envelopes for an unfolded card.

Sources: Office Depot, Office Max for papers and computer supplies

Photo Tip *Paste-up and layout*

You can design your own birthday cards, Christmas cards, or greeting cards from photos in several ways. You can affix an actual photo to a card (project #3), paste-up a collection of photos and photocopy them (project #44), scan the image into your computer (project #45), or use a combination of techniques.

By computer, you can choose whatever style of font you like for the words, use a scanner to put photo images into it, use a software program to design page layouts, and print full-color, archival-quality pieces. You don't need to have skill or all the above equipment.

If you are not up to speed on computer designing, you can paste-up your own layout. To do this, assemble a page of photos and text, then run multiple photocopies. Lacking a color printer, you could even photocopy in black and white, then color the page by hand.

Professionally taken wedding pictures and studio portraits are owned and copyrighted by the photographer. These shots cannot legally be reproduced without the photographer's permission. It's best to take your own shots at a wedding, or borrow some from a friend. These are often more delightfully candid, anyway.

Photo Art & Craft

Photo by Robert Vigiletti

Sylvia Vigiletti makes thoughtful notes by photographing a gift bouquet for thank-you card imagery, 4" x 5 1/2".

Photo by Robert Vigiletti

Sylvia made a note card for a quilt and bear collector.

Scanner cards

Personal notes

Examples by Sylvia Vigiletti and Leslie Masters Villani

Here's a wonderful idea for thank-you notes. While Sylvia Vigiletti recovered, many friends sent her beautiful get-well flower arrangements. Sylvia, an artist to her toes, photographed the flowers against a plain background, scanned the photos into her computer, and created thank-you notes to show the senders their bouquets. Usually she moves the camera in close to feature a single cluster of flowers. On another card, to a child who loves teddy bears, she superimposed the child's face on the bear's head. Use your artist's eye in composing photographs.

You need:
- Photo
- Note card paper stock
- Computer and programs (Adobe Photoshop)
- Scanner
- Printer

Computer-made note cards have several good qualities. Not only can you print full-color cards at home that feature personal photos of family, friends, or scenes, and add text in a variety of fonts, but you can also manipulate the photos. Those skilled on Adobe Photoshop, or a similar graphic program for computers, can import the photographs by scanner and manipulate them in a variety of ways. Use a graphic design program to achieve a remarkably professional looking card with a very personal message.

The abstract imagery for this card came from light reflected through a glass vase that Sylvia blew and formed.

1 Photograph flowers in front of a sheer curtain for a simple background and soft, filtered light (top, previous page). Use flash or flood lights to fill in the foreground. Move in for close-up shots or shoot long-range scenes of nostalgic places.

These cards show extreme close-ups of flowers against dark backgrounds.

2 Scan the photo into your computer. The scanner digitizes the image, putting it into a form you can manipulate. To do this, specify a graphics program, such as Adobe Photoshop, where you can change the size of the photo, intensify or alter colors, add or subtract parts of the photo, and experiment with a variety of effects.

3 In designing your card, consider the envelope. Office supply stores now sell envelopes made especially for 8 1/2" x 11" sheets folded in thirds (business) or in quarters.

4 Design the card's layout according to the way it folds, so the photo is on the front page. The photo on a single-fold card is the lower half of the 8 1/2" x 11" paper. For a double-fold card, the image goes in the lower right quarter of the 8 1/2" x 11" paper. The text appears inside the card (top half, upside down), and your imprint as the card creator appears on the back... just like Hallmark (lower left quarter). Follow instructions for your computer program.

5 Select appropriate paper for your card; use card stock for single fold cards, or use lightweight stock for double folded ones. Many front-loading printers will not accept a stiff card stock, but back or top loading printers will take unusual papers. Print on clear white for the best color, or try colored and textured papers for novelty.

Sources: Epson® high quality ink jet paper

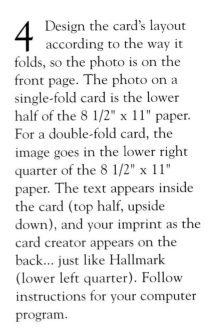

Lindsay Balmer Hinz used her parents wedding photo for imagery on their 50th wedding anniversary party invitations.

The textures and colors—soft gray-purple, muted gray-green and gold—are subtle and elegant.

Matched stationery

By Lindsay Balmer Hinz

Among the senses, touch is as important as sight. The feel of textured thicker papers pleases the fingertips in the same way color and over-all design delight the eye. Elegance is the subliminal dimension of an invitation with heavyweight card stock and graceful lettering. The message is the same as a type-set note on 20 lb. bond typing paper, but the "packaging" makes it special.

Lindsay Balmer Hinz created a matched set of stationery for her parents' 50th wedding anniversary. For her envelopes, she chose a plum-colored, heavyweight paper, die-cut to size. She picked an off-white, color-flecked stock for the invitations, the memory book page, and response card. This paper has matching envelopes commonly available from Office Max. She scanned their wedding picture into her Macintosh computer along with a

You need:

- Photo image
- Soft gray-green fluted card stock
- Off-white color-flecked card stock
- Plum colored paper for envelope
- Sticker paper for computer
- Gold textured paper
- Stamps
- Paper cutter
- Glue

hand-written line of poetry to use as imagery on the invitation. Weeks before the party, she mailed out a request to fill memory pages to go in a book, followed later by the invitations. Finally, she designed coordinated thank-you notes for her folks.

Several developments make it possible for anyone to create such elegant personal mailings, especially if you have a good design eye like Lindsay. First, computers provide a variety of fonts for lettering and page layouts. Second, many computer printers can now print on card stock and textured papers. Third, richly textured papers are available in art stores, office supply stores, and specialty paper stores. All this adds up to your own print shop.

Note: Nonstandard or square envelopes need hand canceling and take more postage.

1 Select a photo related to the event. Scan in the photo, and select a coordinating color. (The subtle plum and soft gray-green are more elegant than the photo shows.)

2 You can design your cards and return envelopes to fit available stock sizes, have the paper company die-cut and fold them to size, or make them yourself. Sizes for the collection shown: 7 1/8" square fluted card stock (Outback by Envelopes), 5 1/2" square off-white card stock, 1 3/4" x 2 1/4" and 2 1/2" x 5" photo images, and irregularly shaped gold paper (art supply stores). For the invitation envelope: 11 1/4" square plum envelope, 5 1/4" x 4 1/4" off-white return card with matching envelope (Star-

dust by Wausau), and 5 1/2" x 8 1/2" off-white memory page with send and return matching envelopes.

3 Design the collection to include three cards—a request for memory pages, an invitation, and a return card. If your computer can't or won't print odd-sized cards, print two invitations on 8 1/2" x 11" paper and trim to size.

4 Print return addresses on the envelopes by computer. Group print the photo images, 18 per page, and cut apart. Group print the photo-image stickers for the envelope on gray-green paper.

5 Spray-mount (outside for ventilation) or glue-stick labels. Glue the photocopied image on the card. Stick stamps on the return envelopes.

6 Mail the memory page and stamped, folded return envelope several weeks early to complete the memory book by event time. Enfold the invitation collection, and apply photo sticker to seal. Hand address or stick on the label, add a pretty stamp, and send.

Sources: www.envelopes.com, Office Max, art supply stores, Fiskars Rotary Paper Cutter

Guests received a CD filled with music of the swing era. Lindsay says that although she has a design business, this project was done from pure love for her parents.

Photo Art & Craft

Photos by Douglas Stroud

The cat portrait and this illustration were both shot in high resolution mode by a digital camera.

Computer screen

Digital camera

Example by Douglas Stroud

So there you are in front of your computer screen. The Balinese people are known to make everything as artistic as possible, without separating art from living. You can too, by scanning a favorite photo and putting it on the computer desktop. With a digital camera you can do it right this moment. The photos for this project were all done digitally.

Digital cameras continue to arrive on the market and improve in ease and quality. You snap the shot, view it on the camera screen to assess quality, and then delete or save. Now it can be downloaded it into your computer, where you can alter and improve the photo. From your computer, digitized images can be put into a newsletter, printed as photos on glossy paper, e-mailed to friends, or put on your computer desktop.

You need:
- Photo and scanner or a digital camera
- Computer

The digital camera has speeded things up photographically and reduced the intermediate steps remarkably. It turns the scene not into a film negative but into a digitized image. Newspapers like this convenience, since they can send the image anywhere in the world electronically and from there to the printed page.

1 Pick a scene you enjoy, one the desktop icons will show up on. You can import and store a collection of photos to change the desktop screen as often as you wish; to suit your mood, for different family members using the computer, or to provide art work in the room while the computer is on.

2 If you have a digital camera, photograph the scene and download it into your computer. Digital cameras come with software programs to plug the camera into the computer and download the images. A great number of photo images can be stored in numbered order. They can be cross-referenced into categories such as family photos, trip to France, etc.

If you don't have a digital camera, you can scan the photo into your computer and display it on the desktop.

3 To enhance and manipulate the images, import photos into various design programs.

───────────

Sources: Digital cameras by Kodak (C 265 Zoom Camera) Olympus, FinePix, and others

Photo by Douglas Stroud

Jessie the cat, foreground, now appears on Bradley Stroud's computer desktop.

Photo Art & Craft

Anyone who missed the photo session can be added later by computer, just as Garrett Hall assembled his friends.

The mock ticket to Garrett and Joan's wedding uses computer-manipulated, borrowed imagery from the University of Michigan football season ticket.

Football fan

Design by computer

Example by Garrett Hall

Once you are up and running with scanning photos into your computer for a variety of uses, you can go to the next step and alter the photographs to suit. A graphics program such as Adobe Photoshop allows for many manipulations such as removing and adding elements. You can "retouch" an image to add lipstick, erase errant wisps of hair, make thinner thighs, and all manner of improvements. If the family picture shows a significant other who is no longer significant, this person can be edited out, and whoever missed the scene can be added.

Another technique involves scanning images onto different cells or layers of imagery. As in movie cartoons, the main character is drawn on the top layer cell and bounces along in front of the background scenic layer. This technique allows for overlaying text or images.

You need:
- Photos or digital camera
- Photoshop computer software program

Three examples show different computer techniques that Garrett Hall likes to use—removing extra details, borrowing imagery, layering images, and adding.

The "Peter & Sandy" note (below) shows removing details. Garrett and cousin Peter Goodrich have a fierce college football rivalry going with this duck trophy going to the yearly winner, hence the gloating note. To make this image (sent by e-mail) the Halls set up the scene on their deck with a drink for Ducky. Good natured as their cat Topper is, he wouldn't wear the sunglasses, so Joan held them (and him) in place while Garrett snapped the photo and scanned it in. Later, Joan's hands were edited out.

Borrowed imagery is used on the small ticket (bottom, previous page). These two alumni created a ticket to their wedding, by scanning imagery from their University of Michigan football season ticket. At the ticket top end, their names were substituted in reversed color, and then the wedding date was added. In the center, a photo of them in blow-up chairs at the Penn State game was inserted. The faux tickets were laminated on both sides to stiffen the paper.

An example of layered imagery appears on their 1999 holiday card (lower right). Topper the cat is playfully added to nearly every scene—wearing a Santa hat, peeping around the mountain, and leaping over the house. He actually does ride on the kayak. For this card, photographs of the year's events were scanned in. Added images of Topper, Ducky, and the band were scanned in and trimmed of background, then placed in the scene. Captions in various type fonts and colors are overlaid. Gare later added hand-written notes.

Friends come and go in the Party Hut at Gare and Joan's tailgate parties, but not all at the same time (top, previous page). To remedy this for the 2000 football schedule, pictures of friends were scanned in, trimmed around the edges, scaled in size to fit, and added into the scene. The cards were laminated onto magnetic backing for refrigerator mounting.

Sources: JM Laminate, Michaels for magnetic backing

Garrett Hall sent this e-mail to his cousin Peter, showing Topper wearing sunglasses. He cleverly edited out his wife, Joan, holding the cat.

Garrett Hall layered photos of their cat Topper onto several unlikely places for their Christmas card.

Art Director Claudia Hall Stroud enjoys making books by computer that tell of special events, such as the trip to China.

Claudia scans in photos of the trip, then composes pages and captions using her computer software programs.

China trip

Making books

By Claudia Hall Stroud

Create books for any occasion—as gifts, to savor special trips, for school projects, or to present other material. For a gift book, select nostalgic family photos and memorabilia. For records, choose the best of photos and memories from a barge cruise or a Boy Scout camping outing. For a PTA report, assemble text and photos to get the message across. Using a computer, it is easy to make multiple copies by printing duplicate pages.

Bypass filling a ready-made album, and manufacture your own books. Books have these basic components: The pages consist of pictures and text telling a story. The front and back covers protect the pages and announce what's in the book. The binding holds the covers and pages together in a flexible manner.

You need:
- Photos
- Computer paper
- Cover stock paper
- Scanner
- Computer
- Staples or spiral plastic or wire binder
- Laminating sheets
- Hole punch, stapler, or paper cutter

Dimensions:
Shown 8 1/2" x 11" horizontal

1 Select scenic photos, text, and photos of objects that tell your story. For a special trip, add close-up photos of souvenirs. For family memories, add certificates, report cards, postcards, or new photos of old familiar places. Once you begin collecting, your problem will be selecting.

2 Put the content—pictures, text, and other material— in order, apportioning it to successive pages.

3 Scan or type the content into your computer to lay out each page. Decide the size of the pages and the orientation, vertical or horizontal. Consult your computer software manuals on procedures for setting text in type and arranging the blocks of type and the photos.

4 Select a good quality paper such as a standard white or an unusual handmade paper that your printer can accept. Use a heavier weight, if you plan to print on both sides, so the printing doesn't "shadow" through. To make the photos glow, use a glossy, photo-quality paper.

5 Choose a cover stock weight of paper (90 pound) for the front and back covers, or print the cover(s) on regular printer paper and clear-laminate them.

6 Several kinds of binding are available, but it's best to plan the binding from the beginning. For the simplest binding, lay out the pages so they fold in the center, then staple or sew along the fold. The 8 1/2" x 14" paper folded would make up into a 7" x 8 1/2" booklet. Use a paper cutter to even the edges and trim to size.

Print shops or office supply stores can bind your book by punching holes and threading through a wire plastic spiral. Or buy a hole punch and spirals to bind your own books. The three-hole punch and three ring notebook combination is the easiest and most flexible for changing pages. Some notebooks have a clear plastic slot for your own imagery on the cover.

Sources: Ibico® binding machines, cover sets and binding combs (the spirals); ACCO® Brand 3-hole punches (electric or hand); Fiskars® or X-Acto paper cutters; Stanley® Bostitch heavy-duty extra long reach staplers.

Old family photos can be made into charming books, especially appropriate as gifts.

Photo Art & Craft

Grandson Bradley oversees the guest book at the autograph party.

Family art

Photo accolades

Congratulations by Claudia Stroud

"Congratulations, Mom..." reads the plant stake in this floral tribute. This wonderfully personal card makes the gift even more special. A card like this mounted on a skewer could be stuck in a plant, on a cake, or in a gift basket of food. Or make one like this with personal imagery for a gift tag, an announcement card, or a thank-you note. The cover of a newly published book is the imagery used here, but anything might apply—a shot of a married couple, a race winner, a special garden, a beloved pet, a new house, or anything else you want to feature.

The plant stake photo is ink-jet printed on glossy photo paper, cut out, and taped to a skewer. This image was laminated to prevent moisture damage.

You need:
- Scanner
- Computer
- Object or photo
- Paper
- JM Laminate
- Skewer
- Tape

1 Select a photo, or scan the object directly into the computer. The book cover was scanned in directly, but a three-dimensional object will need photographing first.

2 Select the size you want the finished image to appear, and import the image into a layout program, such as Adobe Photoshop, PageMaker®, or Illustrator®. QuarkXPress®, an integrated publishing program, combines text, graphics, typography, and printing controls.

3 Write the text, and select a suitable font to carry the visual message—business-like, cheerful, flamboyant, or ponderous. On your computer there will be many fonts (also called type faces). Experiment with them to find what one that suits you.

4 Print photo cards on a glossy paper for snappiest results. Some newer printers have waterproof ink to prevent ink smear (when you water the plant). For an ink jet printer

with water-soluble ink, cover the finished print with clear laminate to avoid smear.

5 Trim the card to size on a paper cutter or with scissors. Tape the skewer on the reverse side with clear tape, and make someone happy with a special gift.

Claudia Hall Stroud created a plant stake congratulations card.

Photo Art & Craft

Homework: The Gramma Poem, by Hattie Stroud

Want to get a sure A+ on your homework? Do it on the computer with a photo scanned into it. Hattie Stroud picked a photo of her grandmother for a visual prod to her creativity and then made sure she met all the requirements of the class assignment—does your poem have a message, real feelings, strong imagery, and use poetic devices such as simile, metaphor, and personification? This writing technique can make wonderful gifts. Let the guests read and show their picture poems as entertainment at an anniversary dinner, birthday party, or retirement roast.

1 Choose the photo and write your poem. Write a poem, limerick, description, or memory related to the photo (or photos). One friend saves news magazines, then writes poems telling current events at noted times in his subject's life such as born on D-Day, married the year Hurricane Andrew blew through Florida, or retired the same year the Berlin Wall came down. Hattie says she just looked at the picture and described Gramma from there.

2 Select an appropriate font in a size to fit the page, here italic. Hattie ran the title across the page top with the photo on the left and text down the right. In asymmetrical balance, the photo and white space balance the vertical text. Your computer can center the text like an invitation, or justify (line up the edge of the type) to the left as is most common, justify to the right for an inventive layout, or justify both sides for neat blocks of text. The fun with a computer is shifting your layout and fine tuning spaces until you get it right.

3 Select a good paper—a plain paper, a photographic glossy surface, stationery with decorative borders, or card stock.

Sources: Office supply stores

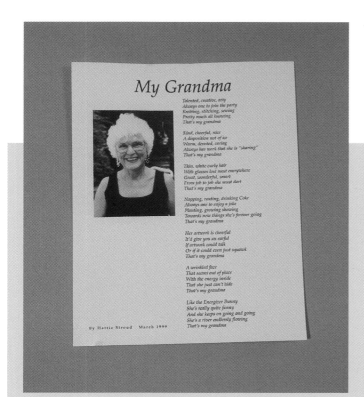

You need:

- Computer (Power Macintosh® used here)
- Scanner (Hewlett Packard used here)
- Software (Adobe Photoshop, QuarkX-Press, etc.)
- Photo image
- Paper
- Frame

Appendix

About Cameras

For different kinds of photos, you may need different cameras, lenses, and films. Most people use one or more of four different kinds of cameras—the point-and-shoot, the SLR, the digital, and the Polaroid.

Point-and-shoot cameras have a small viewfinder to frame the scene. The least expensive have a fixed focal length. Better ones have automatic focusing, built-in flash, variable settings, delayed shooting, and some have a telephoto setting like my little light-weight Olympus Stylus® zoom 140 that shot many photos in this book. For travel, it fits in purse or pocket, or can dangle from the wrist.

In the heavier SLR camera (single lens reflex), you see the scene through the lens itself in actual focus. Different lenses can be snapped onto this camera to achieve different effects. A Macro lens is used for very close shots (up to an inch away), a telephoto lens for bringing distant objects closer—the longer the lens, the closer the object will appear—or a wide angle lens for taking in more scene. These use an auxiliary flash to move the light farther from the lens to avoid flat lighting and red-eye. My Minolta 7000 SLR camera took most of the slides for illustrations.

The new digital cameras with built-in flash and variable settings take photographs the same way—aim the camera at the scene and click the shutter, so the light can enter—but the technology is different. There is no film. The image is electronically digitized and stored on a disk. Download it into your computer to manipulate and print it, or take the disk to the camera or print shop for "hard copy" prints. Doug Stroud's Kodak digital camera took the Computer screen project photos.

The Polaroid camera is an instant camera with a film-developing packet enclosed. Snap the picture and the camera rollers squish the packet to release developer into the picture dyes. In a minute, the picture is developed. Most of these are inexpensive with limited lenses. You can use a Polaroid film pack on a high-end camera like a Haasleblad with a larger format (2 1/4" square negative) for test photos. The Polaroid transfer projects use a Polaroid camera.

Films

Films come in different speeds from 25 to 800. With lots of light, use the lower number, but for dim light or to freeze motion use the high-speed film such as 200-800. Films come as negative to make prints, or positive as slide films for projecting. Slide films are daylight color-balanced for sunlight, or tungsten color-balanced for incandescent lighting such as photofloods. Use daylight film for flash cameras. Some films are color balanced to brighter reds and some to brighter greens. Ask at the camera shop about your film needs.

Hope you have as much fun as I do with photographs.

A seven-year-old boy created this computer-generated scene with grandfather Robert Vigiletti's help.

Photo Art & Craft

Books to Inspire You and Your Family

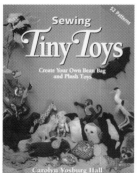

Sewing Tiny Toys
by Carolyn Vosburg Hall

Small plush toys are all the rage, and now you can quickly and easily create your own using such readily available materials as felt, fake fur, beads, ribbons, pipe cleaners, and pellets. Included are patterns for 60 original animals like bears, dogs, and birds, complete with easy-to-follow instructions and clear illustrations.

Softcover • 8-1/4 x 10-7/8 • 144 pages
200 illustrations • 75 color photos
Item# TOZ • $21.95

Year 'Round Fun 2
A Book for All Seasons
edited by Bill Stephani

You can never have too many projects when working with kids. So here's Year 'Round Fun II with even more activities to entertain kids all year long. You'll get full-size patterns, group activities, party ideas, Bible-school projects, plus a bonus cutout ready to clip and glue. They're easy, educational, and inexpensive. You'll want this hands-on book within easy reach to use over and over.

Softcover • 8-1/4 x 10-7/8 • 104 pages
Color throughout
Item# YRF2 • $14.95

Sewing for Your Garden
by Carolyn Vosburg Hall

If you love to sew and garden, this book is a must-have! You will find hours of enjoyment creating any of the 50 innovative, colorful, practical projects like tablecloths, totes, blankets, knee pads, gloves, aprons, centerpieces, and wind socks that will help you dig in the garden, serve lunch on the patio, frolic by the pool, or tailgate at the big game.

Softcover • 8-1/4 x 10-7/8 • 128 pages
180 illustrations and 90 color photos
Item# SGAR • $19.95

The Ultimate Rubber Stamping Technique Book
by Gail Green

Goof-proof methods and clear step-by-step instructions and photos will help you master a wide variety of rubber stamping techniques from masking to mirror imaging. While exploring various surfaces like fabrics, wood, paper, and leather, create more than 130 unique projects such as memory album pages, clothing, greeting cards, picture frames, and giftware.

Softcover • 8-1/4 x 10-7/8 • 144 pages
175 color photos
Item# USTB • $19.95

Year 'Round Fun
edited by Bill Stephani

Everyone who works with kids will love this book filled with inexpensive projects for every occasion! Kids will find exciting projects to make and do from January through December with the quick and easy party ideas, group activities, Bible-school projects and much more. As an added bonus, the book contains an 8-page cutout section featuring the Delta Star X7 Shuttle Lander. It really flies!

Softcover • 8-1/4 x 10-7/8 • 96 pages
96 color photos
Item# YRF • $14.95

Arnold Grummer's Complete Guide to Easy Papermaking
by Arnold Grummer

Arnold Gummer, the foremost papermaking expert in the United States, teaches you basics of papermaking, guides you through over 27 artistic and decorative techniques, plus more special sheets. If you've ever wondered how to achieve a certain effect on paper, you'll find out in this book.

Softcover • 8-1/4 x 10-7/8 • 160 pages
200 color photos
Item# UHPB • $21.95

More Projects to Create Using Photographs

More than Memories
The Complete Guide For Preserving Your Family History
edited by Julie Stephani

Leading scrapbook experts share hundreds of their favorite tips and techniques to instruct and inspire you to create beautiful family albums that will be cherished for generations to come! Clear step-by-step instructions show you how to organize, protect, and display your treasured photos.

Softcover • 8-1/2 x 11 • 128 pages • 225 color photos
Item# MTM • $14.95

Ultimate Scrapbook Guide
by Julie Stephani

The fourth book in the best-selling More than Memories series is here! Master-scrapbooker Julie Stephani answers the most often asked questions about scrapbooking. Included are hundreds of creative scrapbooking ideas and projects, expert tips and advice on a wide variety of techniques.

Softcover • 8-1/4 x 10-7/8 • 128 pages
Color throughout
Item# MTM4 • $19.95

More Than Memories II
Beyond the Basics
edited by Julie Stephani

The second book in the series goes beyond the basics to include step-by-step instructions on photo tinting, paper embossing, and photo transferring, as well as ideas on making greeting cards, puzzles, and time capsules. There are still plenty of great page layout ideas on thirteen favorite themes, including Heritage, Home and Family, Babies, Vacations, Weddings, and much more.

Softcover • 8-1/4 x 10-7/8 • 128 pages
200 color photos
Item# MTMB • $16.95

Memory Crafting: Beyond the Scrapbook
130 Projects to Sew, Stitch & Craft
by Judi Kauffman

Noted crafter Judi Kauffman has created more than 130 ways for you to preserve precious memories in lovely displayable projects that won't be tucked away in a drawer or cabinet. From snow globes and paperweights to jewelry and pillows, each of these projects offers several options and simple techniques using popular techniques.

Softcover • 8-1/4 x 10-7/8 • 128 pages
75 illustrations • 100 color photos
Item# CMSC • $19.95

More Than Memories III
Mastering the Techniques
edited by Julie Stephani

With help from the experts, you can perfect all of the techniques used in scrapbooking to preserve your family history. Each chapter focuses on a technique and uses projects to illustrate the tips and tricks for mastering the specific tools, products and applications. Learn new and better ways for creative cropping, journaling, and rubber stamping. Hundreds of ideas are included to inspire your creativity.

Softcover • 8-1/4 x 10-7/8 • 128 pages
120 color photos
Item# MTM3 • $16.95

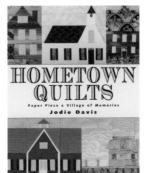

Hometown Quilts
Paper Piece a Village of Memories
by Jodie Davis

Create your own hometown quilt using paper piecing and any combination of the 27 block patterns included in this easy-to-follow book. Complete step-by-step illustrated instructions and full-size patterns are used to teach paper piece quilting, one of the hottest techniques among quilters today. Clear layout diagrams and beautiful color photographs will inspire you to create a quilt from the book, or come up with your own village of memories.

Softcover • 8-1/4 x 10-7/8 • 128 pages
50 color photos
Item# MEMQU • $21.95